SERMONS ON IMPORTANT SUBJECTS

CHARLES FINNEY

W

WHITAKER
HOUSE

Publisher's note:
This new edition from Whitaker House has been updated for the modern reader. Words, expressions, and sentence structure have been revised for clarity and readability. Although the more modern Bible translation quoted in this edition was not available to the author, the Bible versions used were carefully selected in order to make the language of the entire text readily understandable while maintaining the author's original premises and message.

Unless otherwise indicated, all Scripture quotations are taken from the *New King James Version*, © 1979, 1980, 1982, 1984 by Thomas Nelson, Inc. Used by permission. All rights reserved. Scripture quotations marked (KJV) are taken from the King James Version of the Holy Bible.

Sermons on Important Subjects

(Previously published with the title *God in You*)

ISBN: 978-1-60374-571-0

© 1998, 2012 by Whitaker House

Whitaker House
1030 Hunt Valley Circle
New Kensington, PA 15068
www.whitakerhouse.com

This book has been printed digitally and produced in a standard specification in order to ensure its continuing availability.

Contents

Introduction

Charles G. Finney was a man with a message that burned through the religious deadwood and secular darkness of his time. He had the ability to shock both saint and sinner alike. Because he was radical in both his methods and his message, Finney was criticized for almost everything except being boring.

Born in Connecticut in 1792, Finney was nearly thirty years of age before he turned from his skepticism regarding Christianity and wholeheartedly embraced the Bible as the true Word of God. He gave up his law profession in order to spread the Gospel, and he soon became the most noteworthy revivalist of the nineteenth century. It is estimated that over 250,000 souls were converted as a result of his preaching.

Finney's sermons and writings continue to reappear to each new generation of young Christians as a fresh challenge to holiness and spiritual awakening. The sermons collected in the following pages call upon men and women, Christians and non-Christians alike, to examine their hearts in order to avoid hell and reach a fuller, deeper experience of union with God. Each sermon is followed by a number of remarks that reveal Finney's depth of analysis and his spiritual insight into each topic.

The truths presented in this book are ones that Finney deemed crucial to the Christian faith. But far beyond debating topics for the sake of scholasticism, Finney's focus was always upon the hearts of his fellowmen. His wish for all his published works was, "If the Lord can use this little volume to do any good, to His name be all the glory."

One

Sinners Must Change Their Own Hearts

Get yourselves a new heart and a new spirit.
For why should you die?
—Ezekiel 18:31

These words were addressed to Israel, who, according to their history and the passage from which our text verse is taken, were evidently in a state of impenitence. This command to get themselves *"a new heart and a new spirit"* was enforced by the weighty penalty of death. The death mentioned in the text cannot mean natural death, for natural death comes to both those who have and those who do not have a new heart. Nor can it mean spiritual death, which is a state of entire sinfulness, for then the verse would have read, "Why are you already dead?" The death spoken of here must mean eternal death, or the state of banishment from God and the glory of His power. It is the state into which the soul that dies in its iniquities will be cast.

The command here addressed to the Israelites is binding upon every impenitent sinner to whom the Gospel is addressed. Sinners are required to perform the same duty, with the same penalty. Therefore, it becomes a matter of infinite importance that we well understand, and fully and immediately obey, the requirement. The questions that naturally arise when reading the text verse ask the following:

1. What is meant by the requirement to get a new heart and a new spirit?

2. Is it reasonable to require the performance of this duty under the threat of eternal death?

3. How is this requirement consistent with the often repeated declarations of the Bible that a new heart is the gift and work of God? Does God require us to perform this duty, without expecting its fulfillment, merely to show us our powerlessness and dependence upon Him? Does He require us to get ourselves a new heart under the threat of eternal death, when at the same time He knows we have no power to obey and that if ever the work is done, He Himself must do the very thing He requires of us?

In order to answer these questions satisfactorily, I will attempt to show, first of all, what is *not* the meaning of this requirement. Then I will show what is.

What Is Not Meant by Getting a New Heart

Note here that, although the Bible was not given to teach us intellectual ideas, we may rest assured that all its declarations are in accordance with true wisdom. In the Bible, the term *spirit* is used in different senses: it sometimes means a spiritual being or moral agent, while in other places it is used to describe the disposition of a man. In the latter sense, we say a person has a good or bad spirit, a lovely or hateful spirit. The word *spirit* is evidently used in this sense in the text verse: "*Get yourselves a new heart and a new spirit.*"

The term *heart* is also used in various senses in the Bible: sometimes it appears to be synonymous with *soul;* sometimes it evidently means the will, sometimes the conscience; sometimes it seems to be used so extensively as to cover all the moral activities of the mind; and sometimes it refers to a person's natural or social inclinations. In nearly every case, using the context of the word, one may easily determine the particular sense in which it is to be understood. Our task in this chapter is to discover its meaning as it is used in Ezekiel 18:31, for it is in this sense that we are required to get ourselves "*a new heart and a new spirit.*"

I begin, therefore, by saying that *heart* in this case does not mean the fleshly heart or the bodily organ. Nor does getting a new heart mean getting a new soul. We have one soul, and we do not need another. Also, we are not required to create any new physical or mental abilities. We already have all the powers to choose to follow what is moral or what is not; we are just as God made us and do not need any alteration in the substance of mind or body. Nor does this verse mean that we are required to add to our minds or bodies any new principle or inclination. We are not to make any physical change in ourselves.

Some people speak of a change of heart as something miraculous, something in which the sinner is to be entirely passive and for which he is to wait as he would wait for a surgical operation. We need nothing added to our bodies or minds, nor is it true that those who have a new heart have any physical alteration of their powers whatsoever. They are the same people, as far as both body and mind are concerned, that they were before. A physical change, either in body or mind, would destroy a person's identity. A Christian, or one who has a new heart, would not be the same individual that he was before in regard to his powers of moral choice—he would not be the same person having the same responsibilities. The alteration, therefore, lies in the manner in which he uses his moral and physical powers.

A physical alteration in the substance of one's mind would also destroy all the virtue of his obedience. It would make obedience to God a mere gratification of appetite, in which there would be no more real virtue than in eating when we are hungry or drinking when we are thirsty. Think of it: if a principle of holiness were implanted in the mind, it would render the perseverance of the saints physically necessary, make falling from grace a natural impossibility, and would thus destroy all the virtue of perseverance.

Such a thing would also dispense with the necessity of the Holy Spirit after conversion. A re-creation of a person's mental faculties, and the implantation of an inclination toward holiness in the substance of his mind, would plainly dispense with the need for any other power in his life than the power that could keep him alive and give him power to act. For, in obedience to the laws of his renewed nature or in the gratification of his new appetite, he would, of course, obey.

But this implantation of a new principle, which dispenses with the need for the influences of the Holy Spirit after conversion, is contrary to experience in many ways. First, those who have a new heart find that the Holy Spirit's constant assistance is as indispensable to their perseverance in holiness as it was to their conversion. Second, the idea of a physical change is inconsistent with backsliding. If the physical makeup of the mind were changed, if an inclination toward holiness and obedience were implanted in the substance of the soul, then to backslide, or to fall from grace, would be as impossible as to alter the appetites of the stomach.

A physical change is also unnecessary. Some people suppose that the Gospel has no real tendency to move the mind to obey God unless there is a corresponding affinity to do so in the person. In other words, because the influences of the Gospel are holy, there must be something equally holy implanted in the substance of the mind before these influences can act as influences at all. Thus, if the outward influence is holy, there must already be something holy in the person; but if the outward influence is sinful, the person must already have corresponding sinful inclinations.

But this is absurd and contrary to fact. Based on these theories, I must inquire, How did Adam sin? Was it God or the Devil who first implanted a sinful inclination within his physical body as an answer to the outward influence? And how did one third of the holy angels sin? Did God also implant a sinful inclination in their beings? Were Adam and *"the angels who did not keep their proper domain"* (Jude 6) originally created with sinful inclinations that corresponded to those outward influences? Then they were always sinners and were created as such. Who, then, is the author of sin and is responsible for all their wickedness?

It is true, the physical makeup of the mind must be suited and adapted to the nature of the outward influence before the influence can produce any desired action of the mind. And the outward influence must be equally adapted to the mind. Every human being possesses the power to understand, to perceive, and to weigh; he has the power of conscience to decide upon the nature of moral opposites; he has the power and liberty of choice. Now, to the person who possesses these faculties, the influences of the Gospel are directed, and there is plainly a natural tendency in these weighty considerations to influence him to obey his Maker.

If a change of heart were physical, it would have no moral character. In order to have moral character, the change must be voluntary. But no change to the nature of man's soul, no implantation of a craving for obedience to God, could bring him to holiness. All holiness—whether in God, angels, or men—must be voluntary, or it is not holiness at all. To call anything holy that is a part of the mind or body, to speak of a holy substance, unless it is in a figurative sense, is to talk nonsense. Holiness is virtue; it is something that is praiseworthy. Therefore, it cannot be a part of the created substance of the body or mind but must consist in voluntary obedience to the principles of eternal righteousness.

What Is Meant by Getting a New Heart

Now I will show you what we are to understand by the command of our text verse, *"Get yourselves a new heart and a new spirit.*

For why should you die?" The Bible often speaks of the heart as a fountain, from which flow the moral inclinations and actions of the soul, as in Matthew 15:19: *"Out of the heart proceed evil thoughts, murders, adulteries, fornications, thefts, false witness, blasphemies."* The term *heart*, when it is applied to the mind, is figurative, and it recognizes an analogy between the heart of the body and the heart of the soul. The fleshly heart is the seat and fountain of bodily life, and by its constant action, it spreads life through the body. The spiritual heart is the fountain of spiritual life; it is the deep-seated but voluntary preference of the mind that lies behind all its other voluntary inclinations and emotions, and from which they take their character.

The term *heart* is used in the text verse in this latter sense. It is evidently something over which we have control, something voluntary, something for which we are to blame and which we are bound to alter. Now, to require us to make some constitutional change in the substance of our bodies or minds is evidently unjust and is infinite tyranny. The penalty is no less than infinite, yet obedience is impossible. Therefore, it is evident that the requirement here is to change our *moral character*, our moral disposition. In other words, we are to change the abiding preference of our minds that prefers sin above holiness and self-gratification above the glory of God.

A change of heart, as the term is used here, is much like a change of mind. But it is a change in the choice of an *end*, not merely in the choice of *means*. An individual may change his mind and prefer one set of means at one time and another set at another time, to accomplish the same goal, but this does not mean that he has had a change of heart. Let me give you an example. A certain man whose supreme goal in life is his own happiness may, at one time, imagine that his highest happiness lies in the possession of worldly goods. In pursuit of this, he may give himself wholly to the acquisition of wealth, but he may often change his choice of means to this end. At one time, he may pursue merchandise; at another, the profession of law; and still again, the profession of medicine. However, all these are only changes of mind in regard to the means of accomplishing the same selfish end.

Now suppose this same man sees that his happiness does not consist in the abundance of wealth because he has learned that he will exist forever. He now has a higher interest in the things of eternity than in those of time. Therefore, he accordingly enlarges his selfish aims and carries his interests into eternity. He says that his supreme pursuit is now the salvation of his soul. He now seeks an eternal interest instead of a temporal one, but still the end is his own happiness. The end is substantially the same; it is only the exercise of selfishness on a more ample and extended scale. Instead of being satisfied with the happiness of time, his selfishness aims at securing the bliss of eternity.

When confining his views and desires to the acquisition of worldly goods, this man aimed at amassing the services, honors, and wealth of the world. In his pursuit of salvation, he merely "lengthened the cords and strengthened the stakes" (see Isaiah 54:2) of his selfishness, carrying his own aims, desires, and efforts toward eternity. He prayed, read his Bible, became marvelously religious, and eagerly enlisted the powers of all heaven and of the eternal God. While his views were confined to earthly things, he was satisfied that men should be his servants; but then, in the selfish pursuit of his own eternal happiness, he gladly called in all the attributes of Jehovah to serve him. But in all this, there was no change of heart. He may have often changed his choice of means, but his end was always the same; his own happiness was his idol.

A change of heart, then, consists in changing the controlling preference of the mind in regard to the end of one's pursuit. The selfish heart prefers self-interest over the glory of God and the interests of His kingdom. A new heart prefers the glory of God and the interests of His kingdom over one's own happiness. In other words, a new heart is a change from selfishness to benevolence, from having a supreme regard for one's own interests to an absorbing and controlling choice for the happiness and glory of God and His kingdom.

A change of heart is also a change in the choice of a supreme ruler. The conduct of impenitent sinners demonstrates that they prefer Satan as the ruler of the world. They obey his laws, campaign for him, and are zealous for his interests, even to martyrdom. They carry their attachment to him and his government so far as to sacrifice both body and soul to promote his interests and establish his dominion. However, to have a new heart is to choose Jehovah as the Supreme Ruler; it is to have a deep-seated and abiding preference for His laws, His government, His character, and His person, as the Supreme Legislator and Governor of the universe.

Thus, the world is divided into two great political parties. The difference between them is that one party chooses Satan as the god of this world, yields to his laws, and is devoted to his interests, and the other does not. Selfishness is the law of Satan's empire, and all impenitent sinners yield in willing obedience to it. The other party chooses Jehovah for its Governor, and its members consecrate themselves, with all their interests, to His service and glory. People may quit one party and join the other, but this change does not imply a physical alteration of the powers of body or mind, any more than a person's flesh and bones would be altered by a changed outlook on the administration of a human government.

We know by experience that the mind can easily be controlled, in its individual habits and inclinations, by a deep-seated disposition or preference for a particular course or purpose. This fact is illustrated in the story of Adam.

When Adam was first created and awoke into being, before he had obeyed or disobeyed his Maker, he could have had no moral character at all. He had demonstrated no inclinations or desires, and he had not acted on anything. In this condition, he had all the powers of moral choice, but he could not have had any moral character, for moral character is connected to voluntary action.

Most likely, as soon as he awoke into being and had knowledge of the existence and character of his Maker, the evidences of which undoubtedly shone all around him, Adam chose God as his Supreme Ruler and voluntarily dedicated all his powers to the Lord's service. This preference for God, His glory, and His service over Adam's own self-interest and everything else, constituted his disposition, or his moral character. It was a perfectly holy heart. Out of this heart, or preference, flowed the pure waters of obedience. All the subordinate inclinations, choices, and purposes of the mind, and all the outward actions, flowed from this strong and governing preference for God and His service.

Thus Adam went forth to work in God's garden. For a time, this preference in Adam was strong and abiding enough to ensure perfect obedience in all things, for the mind will act in accordance with an abiding preference. For instance, the strong preference that a man may have for home may forbid his entertaining any thoughts of going abroad. The strength of his preference for his wife may prevent his consenting to any improper intimacy with other women. And the probability of his falling into acts of infidelity to his wife depends upon the strength and energy of his preference for her over all other women. Likewise, while the preference of Adam remained unshaken, its energy gave direction and character to all his feelings and to all his conduct.

A strong and continually abiding preference for God and His service is the stamp of perfection upon the obedience of heaven. Indeed, the continued holiness of God Himself depends upon it and flows from the same fountain. Not only is God holy in the substance of His nature, but He also always chooses right. He is immutably holy because He is infinitely strong—so strong and so abiding that He never changes and never displays any conduct inconsistent with His holiness. Adam was perfectly holy, but not infinitely so. As his preference for God was not infinitely strong, it was possible that it might be changed. And we know for a fact that an occasion occurred on which he actually changed it.

Satan, in the form of a serpent, presented a temptation of a very unusual nature. It was addressed to the appetites of both mind and body, to the appetite for knowledge in the mind and for food in the body. These appetites were physical; they were not in themselves sinful, but their unlawful indulgence was sin. The proposal of the Serpent was that Adam should change his mind in regard to his supreme purpose and thereby change his heart, or his whole moral character.

> *"Has God indeed said, 'You shall not eat of every tree of the garden'?" And the woman said to the serpent, "We may eat the fruit of the trees of the garden; but of the fruit of the tree which is in the midst of the garden, God has said, 'You shall not eat it, nor shall you touch it, lest you die.'" Then the serpent said to the woman, "You will not surely die. For God knows that in the day you eat of it your eyes will be opened, and you will be like God, knowing good and evil."*
>
> (Genesis 3:1–5)

The foundation of holiness in Adam, and that which constituted his holy heart, was the supreme choice that God should rule, the supreme preference for God and His glory over his own happiness or self-interest. It is easy to see, therefore, that the objective of the Serpent was to bring about a change in Adam's supreme purpose. This new purpose would be to prefer his own gratification over obedience to his Maker; to become as a god himself instead of obeying Jehovah; to pursue self-gratification instead of the glory of

God. Therefore, in yielding to this proposal, in changing his mind on this fundamental point, Adam changed his own heart and the controlling preference that was the foundation and fountain of all his obedience.

This change in Adam was a real change of heart, from perfectly holy to perfectly sinful. But there was no physical change, no change in the substance of either body or mind. It was not a change in his powers of moral choice themselves, but simply in the use of them; their energies were now directed to a different end. God requires sinners to change their hearts in a similar manner, but from sinfulness to holiness.

Suppose God had come to Adam with the command, "*Get yourselves a new heart....For why should you die?*" Could Adam have justly answered, "Do You honestly think that I can change my own heart? Can I change a heart that is totally depraved?" And might not the Almighty have answered him in words of fire, "Rebel, you have just changed your heart from holiness to sin. Now change it back from sin to holiness"?

Suppose an earthly king establishes a government by which he plans to produce the greatest amount of happiness possible within his kingdom. He enacts laws that are calculated to promote this objective to which he conforms even his own conduct. In the administration of his kingdom, he employs all his wisdom and energies and requires all his subjects to aim for the same objective and to be governed by the same purpose: the promotion of the highest interests of the community. His laws are so constructed that universal obedience to them would result in universal happiness.

Now suppose that one individual, after a time of obedience and devotion to this king, were to withdraw from promoting the public good in order to promote his own happiness. Suppose he were to say, "I will no longer be governed by the principles of goodwill to the community and finding my own happiness in promoting the public interest. Instead, I will aim at promoting my own happiness and glory, in my own way, and will let the king and everyone else take care of themselves."

After he has thus made his own happiness and glory his supreme objective, suppose that he does not hesitate to trample upon the laws and the rights of both his king and his fellowmen wherever those laws or rights lie in the way of accomplishing his goal. It is easy to see that he has become a rebel; he has changed his heart from good to bad. Instead of obeying his king, he has set up an independent sovereignty. Just as Absalom caught the men of Israel and kissed them and thus stole their hearts (see 2 Samuel 15:5–6), so this man now endeavors to enlist the sympathies and command the respect and obedience of everyone around him. The only way this man could have a change of heart toward his king would be for him to go back, change his mind in regard to his main objective, and prefer the glory of his king and the good of the public over his own interests.

This is the case with the sinner. God has established a government and has proposed, by the exhibition of His own character, to produce the greatest possible amount of happiness in the universe. He has enacted laws that are wisely calculated to promote this objective, and He conforms all His own conduct to the same laws to which He requires all His subjects to undeviatingly conform theirs.

After a season of obedience, Adam changed his heart and began to aim for his own glory. So it is with every sinner: although he does not first obey, as Adam did, his wicked heart still consists in setting up his own interests in opposition to God. In aiming to promote his own private happiness, the sinner is opposed to the general good. Self-gratification becomes the law to which he conforms his conduct. In his "minding of the flesh" (see Romans 8:5), he is at enmity with God. A change of heart, therefore, would be to prefer a different end, to prefer the glory of God and the public good over the promotion of his own interests. Whenever this preference is changed, his conduct will change accordingly.

If a man changes sides in politics, he will meet with those who share his views and feelings. He will begin devising plans and using his influence to elect the candidate whom he has now chosen. He has new political friends on the one side and new political enemies on the other. So it is with a sinner: if his heart is changed, you will see that Christians become his friends, and Christ becomes his candidate. The convert aims at honoring Him and promoting His interests in all his ways. Before, the language of his conduct was, "Let Satan govern the world." Now the language of his heart and life is, "Let Christ rule as King of the nations, just as He is King of the saints." Before, his conduct said, "O Satan, let your kingdom come, and let your will be done." Now, his heart, his life, and his lips cry out, "O Jesus, let *Your kingdom come. Your will be done on earth as it is in heaven'* (Matthew 6:10)."

The fundamental difference between a sinner and a Christian lies in this ruling preference, this fountain, this heart, out of which flow their emotions, inclinations, and actions. This difference consists not in the substance of their minds or bodies, but in their voluntary states of mind. Supposing that a physical change has taken place in him who has the new heart is as absurd as inferring that a man's nature has changed because he has changed his politics.

Once the convert's new preference becomes deep enough, the perfection of heaven is stamped upon the whole character. Every act of obedience to God strengthens this preference and renders future obedience more natural. However, when one has been in the habit of sinning and has acted under the dominion of an opposite preference for so long, his change of heart is often weak and inefficient. Consequently, his mind will often act inconsistently with his newfound preference for God. Accordingly, God says to Israel, *"How weak is thine heart"* (Ezekiel 16:30 KJV).

Consider a man who generally prefers his wife over any other woman yet is not deeply influenced by his affection for her. As a result of his weak heart, he may occasionally be unfaithful to his wife. What is needed in the case of a Christian is that his old thoughts, feelings, and habits be broken up; his new preference should gain strength, stability, firmness, and perpetuity and thereby take control of the whole man. This process is called sanctification.

A change of heart is in fact the experience through which every new Christian has just passed. Speaking from experience, he can say, "Though I once preferred my own separate interests over the glory of my Maker, now I prefer His glory and the interests of His kingdom, and I consecrate all my powers to the promotion of them forever."

The Reasonableness of the Requirement

Now let us consider whether the requirement of the text verse, *"Get yourselves a new heart and a new spirit,"* is reasonable and fair. The answer to this question depends on the nature of the duty to be performed. If the change is physical, or if the change is in the substance of the mind, then it is clearly not within the scope of our ability, and the answer to the question must be, No, the requirement is not reasonable and fair. To insist that we are obligated to do what we have no power to do is absurd. If we are under an obligation to do a thing and we do not do it, we sin. Sin is blameworthy because it is the violation of an obligation. But if we are under an obligation to do what we have no power to do, then sin is unavoidable; we are forced to sin by necessity, and then we are bound to repent of it because it is sin. However, it is unreasonable and impossible for us to repent of not doing what we never had any power to do.

Suppose God were to command a man to fly. Would the man be under any obligation until he was furnished with wings? Certainly not. But suppose, when he fails to obey, God were to require him to repent of his disobedience or else be sent to hell. The man would cease to be a reasonable being before he could repent under these circumstances. He knows that God never gave him the power to fly, and therefore God had no right to require it of him. The man's natural sense of justice is outraged, and he indignantly and conscientiously throws back the requirement into his Maker's face. Repentance, in this case, is naturally impossible; while he is a reasonable being, the man knows that he is not to blame for not flying without wings. However much he may regret his not being able to obey, and however great his fear may be of the wrath of God, still it is impossible to blame himself and justify God.

God requires men to make themselves new hearts or else bear the penalty of eternal death. This is the strongest possible evidence that men are able to do it. Their ability is implied in the command itself. Therefore, the reasonableness of the requirement depends upon man's ability to carry it out; and man's ability depends upon the nature of the change itself. If the change is physical, it is clearly beyond the power of man; it is something over which he has no more control than he had over the creation of his mind and body. But if the change is moral—in other words, if it is voluntary, a change of choice or preference, such as I have described—then the answer to the question, Is the requirement of the text just and reasonable? clearly is, Yes, it is entirely reasonable and just. There are three reasons why this is true.

First, every one of us has all the powers of moral choice, and the requirement is not to alter these powers, but to employ them in the service of our Maker. God has created these powers, and we can and do use them. He gives us power to obey or disobey; our sin is that, while He sustains these powers in us, we prostitute them to the service of sin and Satan.

Second, these powers are as well suited to obedience as to disobedience. Is it not as easy to choose right as it is to choose wrong?

Our wickedness consists in a wrong and obstinate choice of sin. Could Adam reasonably have said that he was unable to change his preference and to return to obeying God? Could Satan have objected that he had no power to change the governing preference of his mind—to prefer the glory of his Maker over rebellion against His throne? If we or Satan or Adam can reasonably bring up this objection, then there is no such thing as sin in earth or hell.

Third, God only requires you to choose and act reasonably, for it is certainly in accordance with right reason to prefer the glory of God and the interests of His kingdom over your own interests. It is an infinitely greater good; therefore, you and God and all His creatures are bound to prefer it.

The reasons for choosing right are infinitely greater than for choosing wrong. Sinners often complain that they are so influenced by certain motives that they cannot resist iniquity. They often excuse their sins by pleading that the temptation was too strong for them. Sinner, you claim to be so easily influenced by motives that you cannot resist; you say you are too weak to resist their influence to sin; yet you are strong enough to resist all the reasons that come rolling upon you to do right and obey your Maker. Why is this?

Your mind yields easily to temptation; you are full of weakness and complain that you cannot resist when tempted to disobey God. How can you exert such a giant strength in resisting the infinite weight of reasons to obey God? It is clear that if you did not exert all your powers of moral choice to resist them, these considerations would change your heart.

Who Creates the New Heart, God or Man?

Now we come to the third and last inquiry, which is, How is this requirement, to "*get yourselves a new heart,*" consistent with the often repeated declaration of the Bible that a new heart is the gift and work of God? The Bible ascribes conversion, or a new heart, to four different agents. Oftentimes it is ascribed to the Spirit of God. If you will consult the Scriptures, you will find it still more frequently ascribed to the truth: *"Of His own will He brought us forth by the word of truth"* (James 1:18); *"The truth shall make you free"* (John 8:32); *"Sanctify them by Your truth"* (John 17:17). It is sometimes ascribed to the preacher, or to him who presents the truth: *"He who wins souls is wise"* (Proverbs 11:30); *"He who turns a sinner from the error of his way will save a soul from death and cover a multitude of sins"* (James 5:20). Paul said, *"I have begotten you through the gospel"* (1 Corinthians 4:15). Finally, sometimes it is spoken of as the work of the sinner himself: *"You have purified your souls in obeying the truth"* (1 Peter 1:22), said the apostle. *"I thought about my ways, and turned* [to the Lord]*"* (Psalm 119:59), said the psalmist. *"When You said, 'Seek My face,' my heart said to You, 'Your face, Lord, I will seek'"* (Psalm 27:8), said David.

Now the question is, are all these declarations of Scripture consistent with each other? They are all true; they all mean just what they say, and there is no real disagreement between them. There is a sense in which conversion is the work of God. There is a sense in which it is the effect of truth. There is a sense in which the preacher does it. And it is also the appropriate work of the sinner himself.

The fact is, the actual turning or change is the sinner's own act. The agent who induces him is the Spirit of God. A secondary agent is the preacher or another individual who presents the truth. The truth is the instrument, or motive, that the Spirit or preacher uses to induce the sinner to turn.

Suppose you are standing on the bank of Niagara Falls. As you stand upon the verge of the precipice, you see a man, lost in deep thought, approaching the verge, unconscious of his danger.

He approaches nearer and nearer until he actually lifts his foot to take the final step that will plunge him into destruction. At this moment, you lift your warning voice above the roar of the foaming waters and cry out, "Stop!" The voice pierces his ears and breaks the spell that binds him. He instantly turns around from the verge of death, all pale and aghast. He reels and almost faints with horror as he turns and walks slowly away. You follow him. People begin to surround him as they discover what has happened.

On your approach, he points to you and says, "That man saved my life." Here this man ascribes the work to you, and certainly there is a sense in which you had saved him. But, upon further questioning, he says, "*Stop*—how that word rings in my ears! To me that was the word of life." Here he ascribes it to the word that aroused him and caused him to turn. But, on conversing still further, he says, "If I had not turned at that instant, I would have been a dead man." Here he truthfully speaks of it as his own act. But soon enough you hear him say, "Oh, the mercy of God; if God had not interposed, I would have been lost."

Now, in this case, the only interference God made was a providential one, and the only sense in which God saved the man's life was in a providential sense. But in the conversion of a sinner, there is something more than the providence of God employed. For not only does the preacher cry "Stop!" by the providence of God, but the Spirit of God also cries "Stop!" and forces the truth home upon him with tremendous power. The preacher cries, "*Turn, turn from your evil ways! For why should you die?*" (Ezekiel 33:11). The Spirit then reinforces this with such power that the sinner turns.

Now, in speaking of this change, it is perfectly proper to say that the Spirit turned him. It is also proper to say that the truth converted him. We also may ascribe the change to the preacher or to him who had presented the motives. And the change is also properly ascribed to the individual himself whose heart is changed;

he has changed his mind and has repented. Now, the turning is his own turning, even though God, by the truth, has induced him to turn. Thus it is the work of God and also the sinner's own work. The Spirit of God, by the truth, influences the sinner to change, and in this sense is the efficient cause of the change. But the sinner actually changes and is therefore himself, in the most proper sense, the author of the change.

Some people, after reading their Bibles, see only those passages that ascribe a person's change of heart to the Spirit of God; they seem to overlook those that ascribe it to man and speak of it as the sinner's own act. When they have quoted Scripture to prove it is the work of God, they seem to think they have proved that it is a thing in which man can only be passive. But the requirement of the text verse and the declared fact that God is the author of the new heart are quite consistent with each other. God commands you to *"get yourselves a new heart"* and expects you to do it. Thus, if it ever is to be done, you must do it.

Remarks

1. *Sinners make their own wicked hearts.* Their preference for sin is their own voluntary act. They make self-gratification the rule to which they conform all their conduct. Soon enough, any effort to thwart them in the gratification of their appetites is met with strong resistance; they seem to set their hearts completely on pursuing their own happiness and gratifying themselves, come what will. Thus, they will successively make war on anyone, even family members, whenever they find that others' requirements prohibit the pursuit of this end.

This is purely a voluntary state of mind. This state of mind is not a result of creation; it is entirely the result of natural human selfishness. The preference for selfishness is allowed by the sinner to grow stronger and stronger until his desperately wicked heart bears him onward to the gates of hell.

2. *From what has been said, the necessity of a change of heart is obvious.* All impenitent sinners are in a state of mind that the apostle called *"the carnal mind"* (Romans 8:7), which *"is enmity against God"* (verse 7). God requires sinners to keep their bodies under control, to make their bodies instruments of service to God, and to subject and subordinate all their bodily passions to the will of their Maker. But instead of this, they make the gratification of their appetites and passions the law of their lives. This is the same *"law in [the] members,"* the *"law of sin"* (Romans 7:23), that the apostle Paul spoke of as warring against the law of his mind. This state of mind is the direct opposite of the character and requirements of God. With this heart, the salvation of the sinner is an impossibility.

3. *In this light, you can see the nature and degree of the sinner's dependence on the Spirit of God.* The Spirit's assistance is not needed to give the sinner power, but to overcome his voluntary obstinacy. Some people seem to think that the Spirit is employed to give the sinner power, that the sinner is unable to obey God without the Spirit's help. I am alarmed when I hear such declarations as these. I have already shown that a man is under no obligation to do what he has no ability to do. Therefore, he cannot blame himself for not having exerted a power that he never possessed. If he believes, therefore, that he has no power to obey his Maker, it is impossible for him to blame himself for not doing it. And if he believes that the Spirit's assistance is indispensable to make him able, then he must also believe that, without this assistance, he is under no obligation to obey.

This aid of the Holy Spirit to obey God is sometimes called a *gracious ability,* which is an absurd term. What is grace? It is undeserved favor, something to which we have no just claim and which may be withheld from us without injustice. If this is a true definition, it is clear that a gracious ability to do our duty is absurd. If God requires us to perform any duty or act, justice requires Him to give us the power to obey. But if justice requires this, why call it a gracious ability? Natural ability to do our duty cannot be a gracious ability. To call it such is to imply that grace and justice mean the same thing. The sin of disobedience, in this case, would lie not in breaking the law of God, but in not complying with the striving of the Spirit.

Therefore, while a man does not perceive that the Spirit is giving him power, he can feel under no obligation to be converted; nor can he reasonably blame himself for not being converted. How, based upon these principles, is he to blame for not having repented and turned to the Lord?

Now, allow me to further illustrate man's dependence on the Spirit. Suppose a man wishes to commit suicide. While his wife is out of the room, he loads his gun and prepares to commit the horrid deed. His little child observes his disturbed mind and says, "Father, what are you going to do?"

"Be still," he replies. "I am going to blow my brains out."

The little one weeps, begs his father to stop, and pours out his little prayers, tears, and agonizing entreaties in order to spare his father's life. Now, if the eloquence of this child's prayers and tears could change the obstinacy of the man's purpose, he would need no other influence to change his mind. But when the father persists, the child screams to his mother, who rushes over to see what is wrong. The mother, who is terrified, then urges the man to change his intention.

Over and over again, she urges him not to hurry his own destruction. She reminds him of his love for his family; of their love for him and their dependence upon him; of her own breaking heart; of the anguish, tears, and helplessness of his children; of the regard he has for his own soul; of the hope of heaven and the terrors of hell; of everything tender and persuasive in life. If all this could move him, he would need no other or higher influence to change his mind.

But when she fails in her efforts, suppose that she could then summon all the angels of God, but they also fail to move and melt him by their unearthly eloquence. Here, then, some higher power must interfere, or the man will be lost. But just as he puts his pistol to his ear, the Spirit of God, who knows perfectly the state of his mind and understands all the reasons that have led him to this desperate act, pours such an influence upon his soul that he instantly quails, drops the weapon from his trembling hand, relinquishes his purpose, falls upon his knees, and gives glory to God.

Now, it was the strength of the man's voluntary purpose of self-destruction alone that made the Spirit's help at all necessary in the case. If he had yielded to all the reasons for living that had been presented before, and if they had changed his mind, no intervention of the Holy Spirit would have been necessary. But it was his wickedness and obstinacy that laid the foundation for the Spirit's interference.

This is the sinner's situation. He has set his heart fully upon doing evil, and if the prayers and tears of friends and of the church of God—such as the warning of ministers, the rebukes of Providence, the commands, expostulations, tears, groans, and death of God's dear Son—if the offer of heaven or the threat of hell could overcome his obstinate preference for sin, then the Spirit's assistance would be uncalled for. But because no human persuasion, no reason that man or angel can present, will cause him to turn, therefore the Spirit of God must intervene to shake his preference and turn him back from hell.

The degree of his dependence upon the Spirit is exactly the degree of his obstinacy. If he were only slightly inclined to pursue the road to death, men could change him without calling upon

God for help. But as the strength of his preference for sin grows, it is necessary that the Spirit intervene, or he will be lost. Thus, the sinner's dependence upon the Spirit of God, instead of being his excuse, is what constitutes his guilt.

4. *So, you can see from this subject the nature of the Spirit's assistance.* The Spirit does not act by direct physical contact upon the mind, but He uses the truth as His sword to pierce the sinner's heart. (See Hebrews 4:12.) The motives presented in the Gospel are the instruments He uses to change the sinner. Some have denied the possibility of changing the heart by motives. But the Serpent changed a heart from a perfectly holy to a perfectly sinful one by the power of persuasion. Cannot the infinitely wise God do as much as Satan did? Indeed, to deny this is much like detracting from the wisdom and power of God.

The Scriptures abundantly declare that the Spirit converts sinners by the power of persuasion. *"Of His own will He brought us forth by the word of truth"* (James 1:18) is one of the many declarations upon this subject. This subject is settled by the Bible; it is a subject upon which we are not at liberty to speculate out of our own philosophical theories or to maintain that God intervenes and changes the sinner's heart by direct physical contact, irrespective of truth. When God says, *"Of His own will He brought us forth by the word of truth,"* this settles the question. He has not begotten us in any other manner.

Our Savior said concerning the Spirit, *"When He has come, He will convict the world of sin, and of righteousness, and of judgment"* (John 16:8). This strongly implies the way in which the Spirit helps the sinner. The Holy Spirit is often referred to as the Comforter, from the Greek word *parakletos*. It is the same term that, in the first epistle of John, is rendered *advocate*. The term is there applied to Jesus Christ. John wrote, *"And if anyone sins, we have an Advocate [a parakletos] with the Father, Jesus Christ the righteous"* (1 John 2:1).

In this passage, Jesus Christ is spoken of as the Advocate of men with God. The *Parakletos*, or Comforter, promised by our Savior, is represented as God's Advocate who pleads His cause with men.

The term *"convict"* (John 16:8) is a law term that signifies the summing up of an argument and establishing the sinner's guilt. Thus, the striving of the Spirit of God with men is not a physical scuffle, but a debate; a strife not of body with body, but of mind with mind. From this, it is easy to determine that, in converting the soul, the Spirit uses the truth and not any physical influence upon the mind. Think about it: would an earthly lawyer who had won his case have done so by acting physically on the jury?

5. *It is evident from this subject that, in changing the sinner's heart, God never does what He requires the sinner to do.* Some people, as I have already mentioned, seem inclined to be passive, to wait for some mysterious influence, like an electric shock, to change their hearts. But with this attitude and these views, they may end up waiting until the Day of Judgment, for God will never do their duty for them. The fact is, sinners, that God requires you to turn, and He cannot do for you what He requires of you. It must be your own voluntary act. It is not the appropriate work of God to do what He requires of you. Do not wait for Him to do your duty, but do it immediately yourself, under the threat of eternal death.

If the sinner will ever have a new heart, he must obey the command of Ezekiel 18:31 and get it himself. You may object and say, "Is this not taking the work out of God's hands, and robbing Him of the glory?" No, it is in fact the only view of the subject that gives the glory to God. Some individuals, in their zeal to magnify the grace of the Gospel, entirely oppose it and maintain the sinner's *inability*, and thereby do away with his guilt. Instead of considering him a guilty, voluntary rebel, and worthy of eternal death, they make him a helpless, unfortunate creature, unable to do what God requires of him. Instead of saying that the sinner's unwillingness is his only difficulty, they insist that he is unable, and thus destroy his guilt and, of course, the grace that would be displayed in his salvation.

For what grace can there be in helping an unfortunate individual? If sinners are unable to obey God, they are therefore guiltless in proportion to their inability. But if they are unwilling, if their "cannot" is a "will not," we have already seen that their guilt is in proportion to the strength of their unwillingness, and grace in their salvation must be equal to their guilt. It does not detract from the glory of God that the act of turning is the sinner's own act. The fact is, the sinner never will turn unless God induces him to do it. So, although the act is the sinner's own, the glory belongs to God inasmuch as He caused him to act. If a man had made up his mind to take his own life, would you deserve no credit if you somehow influenced him not to go through with it? Though changing his mind and relinquishing his purpose of self-destruction was his own act, you instigated his turning. Might it not truthfully be said that you had turned him?

6. *The idea that the Spirit converts sinners by the truth is the only view on this subject that honors either the Spirit or the truth of God.* The work of conversion is spoken of in the Bible as a work of great power. I once heard a clergyman speaking on the great powers of God in conversion. Although he appeared to view conversion as a physical alteration of the body and mind of man, as the implantation of a new principle or inclination, he continued to assert that converting a sinner was a greater exertion of power than that which created the heavens. He claimed that this was such a great exertion of power because, in the creation of the material universe, God had no opposition, but in the conversion of a soul, He has all the powers of hell to oppose Him.

This is whimsical and ridiculous, as if the opposition of hell could set up any obstacle in the way of physical Omnipotence.

But the power that God exerts in the conversion of a soul is moral power, not physical power. It is the kind of power by which a statesman sways the mind of a senate or by which a lawyer moves the heart of a jury. It is distinctly the power by which David *"swayed the hearts of all the men of Judah, just as the heart of one man"* (2 Samuel 19:14). When we consider the deep-rooted selfishness of the sinner, his long-cherished habits of sin, and his multifarious excuses and *"refuge[s] of lies"* (Isaiah 28:17), it is a sublime exhibition of wisdom and of moral power to pursue him step-by-step with truth and to chase him from his lies until, by the force of argument alone, he yields up his selfishness and dedicates himself to the service of God. This reflects a glory and a luster over the truth of God and the position of the Holy Spirit that at once delights and amazes the beholder.

7. *The idea that the Spirit uses persuasive arguments to change the sinner's heart is the only view that is consistent with and gives meaning to the often repeated command not to resist the Holy Spirit.* For if the Spirit operated upon the mind by direct physical contact, the idea of effectively resisting physical Omnipotence would be ridiculous. The same thought applies to those passages of Scripture that caution us against grieving and quenching the Spirit.

8. *You can see from this subject that a sinner, under the influence of the Spirit of God, is just as free as a jury under the arguments of a lawyer.* It is important that we see this point correctly. Suppose a lawyer, while addressing a jury, does not expect to change their minds by anything he says, but waits for an invisible and physical power to be exerted upon them by the Holy Spirit. And suppose, on the other hand, that the jury thought that they must be passive while deciding their verdict, and must wait for a direct physical force to be exerted upon them. In vain the lawyer might plead, and in vain the jury might hear, for until he presses his arguments as if he were determined to affect their hearts, and

until they make up their minds and decide the verdict, both his pleading and their hearing are in vain.

Likewise, if a minister preaches to sinners who believe that they have no power to obey the truth and who are under the impression that a direct physical influence must be exerted upon them before they can believe, he preaches in vain and they hear in vain, for they are still in their sins. (See 1 Corinthians 15:17.) They sit and quietly wait for some invisible hand to be stretched down from heaven and to perform some surgical operation, infuse some new principle, or implant some physical inclination, after which they suppose they will be able to obey God. Ministers should labor with sinners, as a lawyer does with a jury. The sinner should weigh the arguments of the minister and make up his mind as if he were under oath and his life depended upon it. And then he ought to give a verdict on the spot, according to the evidence.

But here one might ask, "If truth is the instrument of converting the sinner, why will he not be converted in hell, where it is said that all the truth will burst upon his mind in all its burning reality?" In answer to this, I conclude that the argument that on earth could have turned the convicted rebel to God will be lacking in hell. When the sinner on earth is crowded with conviction and is ready to fall into despair, ready to flee and hide himself from the presence of his Maker, he is met with the offer of reconciliation. This, together with the other arguments that are weighing like a mountain upon his mind, sweetly bring him to yield himself up to God. But in hell, the offer of reconciliation will not arise; the sinner will be in despair and will have no chance to turn his heart to God.

Suppose a man so completely ruins his fortune that he has no hope of retrieving it. In this state of absolute despair, no argument can reach him to make him put forth an effort. Suppose his reputation is so completely gone that he has no hope of retrieving it. In this state of despair, there is no possibility of reclaiming him; no motive can reach him and call forth an effort to redeem his character, because he is without hope. Likewise, in hell, the poor, dying sinner will be shut up in despair; his character will be gone; his fortune for eternity will be lost. There will be no offer, no hope, of reconciliation, and punishment will only drive him further and further from God forever and ever.

"But," someone may again object, "if a correct understanding of truth presented by the Spirit of God converts a sinner, does it not follow that his ignorance is the cause of his sin?" I answer no. If Adam had continually reminded himself of the truth that he knew, he would have resisted the temptation presented to him. But he allowed his mind to be diverted from the reasons for obedience to the motives for disobedience, and he failed. When he had fallen and selfishness had become predominant, Adam was averse to knowing and weighing the arguments for turning again to God. If he was ever turned, the Spirit of God must have persuaded him.

So it is with every sinner: he sins against the knowledge that he has by overlooking the reasons for obedience and by yielding himself up to the motives for disobedience. Then, once he has adopted such selfishness, his ignorance becomes willful and sinful. Unless the Spirit of God induces him, he will not see. He knows the truth to a sufficient extent to leave him without excuse, but he will not consider it and let it have its effect upon him.

But it may still be asked, "Is it not true, after all, if a full knowledge of truth is all that is necessary to subdue the sinner, that he only needs to know the true character of God to love Him, and that his enmity against God arises out of the sinner's false notions of Him? Is it not true that what he hates is actually the false character of God?" No, he hates the true character of God. He hates God for what He is, not for what He is not. The sinner's character is selfishness; God's character is benevolence. These are eternal opposites. The sinner hates God because God is opposed to his selfishness. While the man remains selfish, it is absurd to say that he is reconciled to the true character of God.

"But is not his ignorance the cause of his selfishness?" No, he knows better than to be selfish. He does not consider the unreasonableness of selfishness, nor will he consider it unless compelled by the Holy Spirit. The work of the Holy Spirit consists not merely in giving instruction, but also in compelling him to consider truths that he already knows—to think about his ways and turn to the Lord. The Spirit urges upon the sinner's mind those arguments that he hates to consider and feel the weight of. It is probable, if not certain, that if all the reasons for obedience had been considered by Adam, or by any other sinner, he would not have sinned. But the fact is, sinners do not think about the truth they know, but they divert their attention and rush on to hell.

The apostle viewed the subject in this light: in speaking of sinners, he said,

> *Having their understanding darkened, being alienated from the life of God, because of the ignorance that is in them, because of the blindness of their heart.*   (Ephesians 4:18)

It is indeed the pressing of truth upon the sinner's consideration that causes him to turn. But it is not true that he is ignorant of these truths before he thus considers them. He knows he must die, that he is a sinner, that God is right and he is wrong, that there is a heaven and a hell; but, as the prophet said, *"They will not see"* (Isaiah 26:11), and, *"My people do not consider"* (Isaiah 1:3). The Spirit's position, then, is not only to instruct, but also to lead the sinner to think about his ways.

But here someone may say, "Isn't this view of the subject inconsistent with the mystery of which Christ spoke when He said, '*The wind blows where it wishes, and you hear the sound of it, but cannot tell where it comes from and where it goes. So is everyone who is born of the Spirit'* (John 3:8)? I have always considered this subject of a new heart as a very mysterious one, but you make it very plain. How is this? Did not Christ say that it was mysterious?" In answer to this, I would ask, Where in that verse does Christ present the new birth as a mystery? The effects that the Spirit produces are matters of experience and observation, and the methods He uses are often revealed in the Bible. But the mystery lies in the manner of the Spirit's communicating with the mind.

We are unable to say how disembodied spirits communicate with each other, or how a spiritual being can communicate with one in the body. We know that we communicate with each other through our bodily senses. The particular manner in which the Spirit of God carries on His debates with the mind is what, in this life, we will probably never know. Nor is it important that we should. Every Christian knows that, in some way, the truth was held before him and pressed upon him until he had to yield. These are matters of experience. But the particular manner in which the Holy Spirit did this is just as mysterious as millions of other facts that we daily witness but cannot explain.

But here, perhaps, another objection may arise: if the sinner is able to convert himself, why does he need the Spirit of God? Suppose a man owes you one hundred dollars and is able but unwilling to pay you. You therefore prepare to sue him, to force him to pay his debts. Now suppose that he says, "I am perfectly able to pay this hundred dollars, so why this lawsuit?" The answer is, "To make you willing to pay, not just able to pay." It is the same with the sinner: he is able to do his duty but is unwilling. Therefore, the Spirit of God plies him with persuasive arguments to make him willing.

9. *Sinners should not be content with simply praying for a new heart.* When sinners have inquired what they should do to be

saved, it is common for some people to tell them to pray that God will change their hearts instead of commanding them to make new hearts. They have used language like the following: "You must remember that you are dependent on God for a new heart. Do not attempt to do anything in your own strength. Read your Bible, use the means of grace, call upon God to change your heart, and wait patiently for the answer."

A few years ago, a lawyer under deep conviction of sin came to my house to inquire what he should do to be saved. He informed me that when he was in college, he and two others were deeply anxious for their souls. They went to the president of the college and inquired what they should do. His directions were, briefly, that they should read their Bibles, keep clear of vain company, use the means of grace, and pray for a new heart, and that before long they would either be converted or would give up reading their Bibles and using such means for their salvation.

When I asked this lawyer how the matter ended, he replied that it turned out as the president told them it would: they soon gave up reading their Bibles. He said that the directions of the president relieved his mind, and that the more he prayed and used the means, the less distress he felt. He thought he was doing his duty, and the more he read his Bible and prayed, the more acceptable he thought he was becoming to God, and the more likely to be converted.

The more diligent he was in using the means of salvation, however, the more self-complacent and contented he also became; and thus he prayed and waited for God to change his heart until his convictions had entirely worn away. With a burst of grief, he added, "Thus it turned out for all of us. The other two are confirmed alcoholics, and I have nearly ruined myself by drink. Now, if there is any hope in my case, tell me what I must do to be saved." When I told him that he must repent immediately, he, as it appeared, yielded himself up to God on the spot.

The advice of the president was just the kind that would please the Devil. It would fulfill his purpose infinitely better than to have told them to abandon all thoughts of religion at once, for this would have shocked and frightened them; as anxious as they were for their souls, they would have turned with abhorrence from such advice. But setting them upon this sanctimonious method of praying and waiting for God to do what He required of them was soothing to their consciences. Another requirement was substituted in the place of the command of God, fostering their spirit of delay, confirming them in self-righteousness. One of two results was to be expected: they would embrace either a false hope or no hope at all.

Since their duty was to pray, to use the means of grace, and to wait for God, it was perfectly natural and reasonable for them to suppose that they were growing better because they were doing what God required of them. The more diligent they were in their impenitent endeavors, the more they believed they could safely rely upon God's converting them. Therefore, the further they proceeded in this way, the less knowledge they had of themselves, their danger, and their deserved punishments; and the more certainly did they grieve away the Spirit of God.

Oh, sinner, instead of waiting and praying for God to change your heart, you should at once summon up your powers, put forth the effort, and change the governing preference of your mind. But here someone may ask, "Can the carnal mind, which is enmity against God, change itself?" (See Romans 8:7.) The original version of Romans 8:7 reads, "The minding of the flesh is enmity against God." This minding of the flesh, then, is a choice or preference to gratify the flesh. Now, it is indeed absurd to say that a choice can change itself; but it is not absurd to say that the agent who exercises this choice can change it. The sinner who minds the flesh can change his mind and can follow God.

10. *From this subject, it is shown that the sinner's obligation to make for himself a new heart is infinite.* Sinner, your obligation to love God is equal to the excellence of His character, and your guilt in not obeying Him is of course equal to your obligation. You cannot for an hour or a moment put off obeying the command-ment in Ezekiel 18:31 without deserving eternal damnation.

11. *You can see that it is most reasonable to expect sinners, if they are to be converted at all, to be converted under the voice of a living preacher or while the truth is presented to their minds.* Many people in the church accept the idea that sinners must have a long season of conviction and that sudden conversions are of a suspicious char-acter. But certainly "this persuasion does not come from Him who calls you" (Galatians 5:8). Nowhere in the Bible do we read of cases of extended conviction. Peter was not afraid on the Day of Pentecost that his hearers did not have enough conviction. He did not tell them to pray and labor for a more impressive sense of their guilt and wait for the Spirit of God to change their hearts. Instead, he told them of their immediate duty. If he had allowed them to escape, to go from under his voice while still in their sins, it is probable that hundreds, if not thousands, of them would not have been converted at all.

It is reasonable to expect the sinner to turn, if he does it at all, while listening to the arguments of a living preacher, just as it is reasonable to expect a juror to be convinced and to make up his mind under the arguments of the lawyer. The lawyer expects that the jurors, if they are to be convinced at all, will be so while he is addressing them. It is absurd to think that it is more likely they will be convinced and will decide their verdict in his favor when they have gone and calmly considered the subject. His purpose is to convince them so completely that he gets their intellects, con-sciences, and hearts to embrace his views of the subject. In this respect, *"the children of this world are in their generation wiser than the children of light"* (Luke 16:8 KJV).

And now, sinner, if you go away from this book without making up your mind and changing your heart, it is most probable that your mind will be diverted. You will forget many things that you have read; many of the arguments and considerations that now press upon you may be removed from your mind; you will lose the clear view of the subject that you now have; and you may grieve the Spirit, delay repentance, and run with unbroken footsteps to the gates of hell.

You see, then, the importance of presenting truth in ways that are calculated to induce the sinner to change his heart. The Spirit always uses considerations that are meant to disarm the sinner, to strip him of his excuses, answer his objections, humble his pride, and break his heart. Preachers should acquaint themselves with sinners' *"refuge*[s] *of lies"* (Isaiah 28:17), and as far as possible take into consideration their whole history, including their present views and states of mind. He who deals with souls should carefully study the workings of the mind and prayerfully adapt his matter and his manner to the condition in which he may find the sinner at the time. He should present his subject in a way that will have the greatest tendency to subdue the rebel at once. If men would act as wisely in attempting to make men Christians as they do in attempting to sway them on other issues, converts would be added to the Lord like drops of the morning dew. If the whole church and the whole ministry had the right views on this subject, if they had the right spirit and would "go forth weeping, bearing precious seed," they would soon reap the harvest of the whole earth and would "return bearing their sheaves with them." (See Psalm 126:6.)

It is of inconceivably great importance that we rightly understand that God converts souls by persuading them with reasons for obedience. Those who do not recognize this truth in their practice, at least, are more likely to hinder than to aid the Spirit in His work. Some have denied this truth in theory but have happily admitted it in practice. They have prayed and preached and talked as if they expected the Holy Spirit to convert sinners by the truth. In such cases, notwithstanding their theory, their practice was acknowledged and blessed by God.

But a lack of attention to this truth in practice has been the source of great error in the management of revivals and in dealing with anxious souls. Much of the preaching, conversation, and exhortation has been irrelevant, perplexing, and mysterious. Sufficient effort has not been put forth to avoid diverting people's attention. Sinners have been kept under conviction for too long because their spiritual guides withheld particular truths that at the time they desperately needed to know. They have been perplexed by abstract doctrines, metaphysical subtleties, and absurd discourses on God's sovereignty, man's inability, and physical depravity and regeneration. Then, discouraged by the contradiction and absurdity from the pulpit, their agonized minds have dismissed the subject as altogether incomprehensible, and they have given up the performance of duty as impossible.

12. *From this subject, you may see the importance of urging upon the sinner every argument and every consideration that can have any weight.* Sinner, while the subject is before you, will you not yield? To keep yourself away from the motives of the Gospel by neglecting church and neglecting your Bible will prove fatal to your soul. And to be careless when you do attend, or to hear yet refuse to make up your mind and yield, will be equally fatal. And now, *"I beseech you therefore, brethren, by the mercies of God, that you present your bodies a living sacrifice, holy, acceptable to God, which is your reasonable service"* (Romans 12:1). Let the truth take hold of your conscience. Throw down your rebellious weapons. Give up your *"refuge[s] of lies"* (Isaiah 28:17). Focus your mind steadfastly upon the considerations that will instantly cause you to accept the offer

of reconciliation while it now lies before you. Another moment's delay, and it may be too late forever. The Spirit of God may depart from you, the offer of life may be made no more, and this last slighted offer of mercy may close up your account and seal you over to all the horrors of eternal death.

Take this to heart, sinner. I beg you to obey the word of the Lord: "*Get yourselves a new heart and a new spirit. For why should you die?*"

Two

How to Change Your Heart

Get yourselves a new heart and a new spirit.
For why should you die?
—Ezekiel 18:31

In the first chapter, I attempted to show you that making ourselves a new heart and a new spirit does not mean that we have to get a new bodily organ or a new soul. Nor does it mean that we are required to implant any new principle in the substance of either our minds or our bodies. I endeavored to show that a change of heart is not something in which a sinner is passive, but in which he is active. The change is not physical, but moral. It is a change in the governing preference of his mind, which consists in preferring the glory of God and the interests of His kingdom over his own happiness and everything else. It is a change from a state of selfishness to a benevolence that prefers God's happiness and glory over his own personal happiness.

Then I attempted to establish the reasonableness of this duty by showing that the sinner is able to change himself and has many reasons to do so.

Finally, I showed that there is no inconsistency between this and the Scriptures that declare a new heart to be the gift and work of God.

This discussion naturally leads us to deal with how the sinner is to change his own heart. We can hear the sinner saying, "How will I perform this duty and change my own heart?" This is an inquiry often made by anxious sinners when they are commanded to change their hearts and are convinced that it is their duty to do so under threat of the dreadful consequences of neglecting to obey. They anxiously inquire, "How will I do it? By what process of thought or feeling is this great change to be brought about in me?"

My goal here is to help you out of this dilemma; to remove, if possible, the darkness from your mind; to clear up what seems to you to be so mysterious; to hold the lamp of truth directly before you; to pour its blaze full upon your path, so that if you stumble and fall, your blood will be upon your own head.

How the Heart Cannot Be Changed

Let me tell you the ways in which you cannot change your heart. First, you cannot change it by working your imagination and feelings into a state of excitement. Sinners often suppose that they must experience great fears and terrors, or that they must bear all the excitement that they are capable of bearing, before they can experience a change of heart. They are led to this belief by a knowledge that such feelings often do precede this change. But, sinner, you should understand that this highly excited state and these fears and horrors are the result of either ignorance or obstinacy, and sometimes of both.

It often happens that sinners will not yield and change their hearts until the Spirit of God has driven them to extremity, until the thunders of Sinai have been rolled in their ears and the lurid fires of hell have flashed in their faces. All this is no part of the work of making a new heart, but it is the result of resisting the performance of this duty. These terrors are by no means essential to its performance, but are rather an embarrassment and a hindrance.

Suppose that, because just one of your children had refused to obey until driven to extremities, all your children believe that they cannot obey until they not only are threatened with severe punishment but also see the rod uplifted. It is the same with sinners.

Must all sinners experience horrors of conscience and fears of hell because, in some instances, a few sinners have experienced such things before they would yield and change their hearts? If you are willing to do your duty when you are shown what it is, such fears and terrors of the mind are wholly unnecessary. God has no delight in such methods for their own sake, and He causes them only when driven to necessity by a person's obstinacy. And when sinners are obstinate, God often sees it unwise to produce these great terrors, and will sooner let the sinner go to hell without them.

Second, you cannot change your heart by attempting to force yourself into a certain state of feeling. When sinners are called upon to repent and give their hearts to God, it is common for them to make an effort to feel emotions of love, repentance, and faith before they will act. They seem to think that all religion is made up of highly excited emotions or feelings, and that these feelings can be called into existence by a direct effort of the will. They spend much time in prayer for certain feelings, and make many agonizing efforts to call into existence those high emotions and feelings of love for God of which they hear Christians speak.

But these emotions can never be brought into existence by a direct effort to feel them. They can never be made to glow and burn in the mind at the direct bidding of the will. The will has no direct influence over the emotions but can only bring them into existence through the medium of our attention—that is, through what we are drawing our attention to or focusing on. Our emotions are dependent upon our thoughts and arise spontaneously in our minds when our thoughts are intensely focused.

Thoughts are under the direct control of the will. We can direct our attention and thoughts to any subject, and corresponding emotions will spontaneously arise in the mind. If a hated subject is under consideration, emotions of hatred will arise. If an object of terror, of grief, or of joy occupies the thoughts, the corresponding emotions will of course arise in the mind with a strength corresponding to the intensity of our thoughts upon that subject. Thus our feelings are only indirectly under the control of the will. They are sinful or holy only as they are thus indirectly called into existence by the will.

Third, you cannot change your heart by monitoring the present state of your feelings. When people are called upon to change their hearts, it is very common for them to turn their thoughts inward, to see whether they possess the proper feelings, whether they have enough conviction, and whether they have the emotions that they think must precede a change of heart. They direct their attention away from the things that are meant to sway their wills, and they think of their present feelings instead. In this diversion of their minds, they inevitably lose what feelings they have, and for the time being render a change impossible.

Our present feelings are part of our awareness; they have a felt existence in the mind; but if, for a moment, they are made the subject of one's attention, they cease to exist. While our thoughts are earnestly focused upon objects outside of ourselves, upon our past sins, upon the character or requirements of God, upon the love or sufferings of the Savior, or upon any other subject, corresponding emotions will exist in our minds. But if we turn our attention to our present feelings and attempt to examine them, there is no longer anything left to cause us to feel, and our emotions cease.

Therefore, instead of waiting for certain feelings or making your present state of mind the subject of attention, be careful to take your thoughts away from your present emotions and to give your undivided attention to some of the reasons for changing your heart.

What Needs to Be Changed

As I have shown, to change your heart is to change the governing preference of your mind. The most important things are that your will is influenced toward what is right, that you reject sin, and that you prefer God and obedience to Him above everything else. The question is, then, How is your will to be thus influenced? By what process is it reasonable to expect to influence your mind in such a way? Until your will is right, it is futile to expect to feel emotions of true love for God, of repentance, and of faith. These feelings, after which you may be seeking and into which you are trying to force yourself, need not be expected until the will is bowed, until the ruling preference of the mind is changed.

And here you ought to understand that there are three classes of motives that decide the will. The first are those that are purely selfish. Selfishness is the preference of one's own interest and happiness over God and His glory. Whenever the will makes a choice under the influence of selfishness, the choice is sinful, for all selfishness is sin.

A second class of motives that influence the will are those that arise from self-love. Self-love is man's inherent dread of misery and love of happiness, and whenever the will is influenced purely by considerations of this kind, its decisions either have no moral character at all, or they are sinful. The human desire for happiness and dread of misery are not in themselves sinful, and the consent of the will to lawfully gratify them is not sinful. But when the will consents, as in the case of Adam and Eve, to a prohibited indulgence, it then becomes sinful.

A third class of motives that influence the will are connected with conscience. Conscience is the judgment that the mind forms of the moral qualities of actions. When the will is decided by the voice of conscience, or a regard to right, its decisions are virtuous. When the mind chooses what is right, then, and only then, are its decisions according to the law of God.

The Bible never appeals to man's inherent selfishness, but it often addresses self-love, or the innate hopes and fears of men, because self-love is not sinful in itself. When the Bible appeals to the hopes, fears, and conscience of mankind, even the minds of selfish individuals are led to investigate the duty of obedience to God. This prepares the way for their consciences to be enlightened. Individuals may investigate this duty while they are still under the principles of self-love, but it is not their inherent hopes and fears that finally and ultimately settle their minds upon obedience to God.

The decision of the will, or the change of preference in the heart, is made, not mainly because at that instant a person hopes to be saved or fears to be damned, but because to act in this manner is right. To obey God, to serve Him, to honor Him, and to promote His glory is reasonable, right, and just. This is a virtuous decision; this is a change of heart. It is true that the offer of pardon and acceptance has a powerful influence on the sinner, because it more fully demonstrates the unreasonableness of rebellion against such a God. But while in despair, the sinner would rather flee than submit. The offer of reconciliation, on the other hand, negates the influence of despair and gives the conscience its greatest power.

Things to Be Considered

Remember, my objective here is to induce you to choose what is right by leading you to a full understanding of your obligations. The following are some considerations intended to induce a change of heart.

The Hatefulness of Selfishness

First, consider the unreasonableness and hatefulness of selfishness. Selfishness is the pursuit of one's own happiness as a supreme good. This, in itself, is inconsistent with the glory of God and the greatest good of His kingdom. You must admit that you have always, directly or indirectly, aimed at promoting your own happiness in all that you have done; that God's glory and happiness and the interests of His kingdom have not been the leading force of your life; and that you have not served God, but have served yourself.

But your individual happiness is of trifling importance when compared to the happiness and glory of God and the interests of His kingdom. Therefore, to pursue your own happiness as your highest good is to prefer an infinitely less good to an infinitely greater good, simply because it is your own. Is this virtue? Is this benevolence? Is this loving God supremely, or your neighbor as yourself? No, it is exalting your own happiness into the place of God; it is placing yourself at the center of the universe, and an attempt to cause God and all His creatures to revolve around you as your satellites.

If you were to succeed in pushing your selfish aims, you would ruin the universe. A selfish being can never be happy until his selfishness is fully gratified. It is certain, therefore, that only one selfish being can ever be fully gratified. Selfishness aims at taking hold of all good for oneself. Give a selfish man a township, and he desires a state; give him a state, and he longs for a nation; give him a continent, and he cannot rest without the world; give him a world, and he is distraught if there is nothing more to gain. Give him all authority on earth, and while there is still a God to rule the universe, his selfish heart will be filled with insatiable desire, until the world, the universe, and God Himself are prostrate at his feet. His ambition cannot be satisfied; his selfish heart cannot rest. If, therefore, you could succeed in your selfish aims, your success would injure, if not ruin, everybody else.

Is this right? Even if you could succeed in subduing the universe to yourself, your happiness would still not be obtained, for a selfish individual cannot be happy. If you could ascend the throne of Jehovah, if you could wield the scepter of universal government, if you could take hold for yourself the honor and the wealth of the entire universe, if you could receive the obedience of God and all His creatures, the very elements of your nature would still be outraged, and your conscience would condemn you. While you were engaged in the exercise of selfishness, the very laws of your moral constitution would mutiny; self-accusation and reproach would fester in your heart, and, in spite of yourself, you would be forced to abhor yourself.

Not only would you hate yourself, but everyone else would also hate and despise you in your selfishness. It is impossible for a person to be happy when he is aware of being deservedly hated and despised. The love of praise is a law of our nature; it is placed in the mind by the Hand that formed it. It is in vain, therefore, for you to expect to be happy in the exercise of selfishness. God, angels and saints, wicked men and devils, the entire universe would be conscientiously and heartily opposed to you while you sustained that character. Your own conscience would give forth the verdict that you deserved their hatred, and it would pronounce you unfit for any other world than hell.

The Guilt of Selfishness

Second, consider the guilt of selfishness. It will be to no credit of yours if there is a bit of virtue or happiness in the universe. If your example were to have its natural influence and were not counteracted by God, it would, like a little leaven, leaven the whole lump. (See 1 Corinthians 5:6.) If all your acquaintances copied your example, and their acquaintances theirs, and so on, you can easily see that your influence would soon destroy all benevolence in the world and would introduce universal selfishness and rebellion against God. It will be no thanks to you if there is an individual in the universe who respects the government of God. You have never obeyed it, and all your influences have been against it. If God had not constantly used countermeasures, His government would long since have been demolished, and virtue, obedience, and love for God and man would have been banished from the world.

Your selfishness has tended to establish forever the dominion of Satan over men. Selfishness is the law of Satan's empire. You have hitherto perfectly obeyed it; and as example preaches louder than words, you have used the most powerful means possible to induce all mankind to obey the Devil. If God has a virtuous follower on earth, if all men are not in league with hell and shouting forth, "O Satan, live forever!" it is no thanks to you, for the tendency of your conduct has been to produce this horrible result.

Again, it is no thanks to you if all mankind are not forever lost. You have done nothing to save them. Your whole life has had a natural tendency to destroy them. Your neglect and contempt of God have exerted the strongest influence within your power to lead them in the way to death. You have done nothing to save yourself, and, by neglecting your own soul, you have virtually said to all around you, your family and friends, to all who are near and far, "Who is the LORD, that [we] should obey His voice?" (Exodus 5:2), or "What profit do we have if we pray to Him?" (Job 21:15). You need not thank yourself, nor expect the thanks of God or of the universe, if any soul from earth is ever saved.

Consider the guilt of this. The guilt of any action is equal to the evils that it produces. Your selfishness has the natural tendency to ruin the world, to destroy God's government, to establish Satan's, and to people hell with all mankind.

The Reasonableness of Benevolence

Third, consider the reasonableness of benevolence, or of loving your neighbor as yourself. Benevolence is goodwill. Benevolence toward God is preferring His happiness and glory over all created good. Benevolence toward men is having the same desire for their happiness as we have for our own. Benevolence toward God, or the preference of God's happiness and glory, is right in itself, because His happiness and glory are infinitely the greatest good in the universe. He prefers His own happiness and glory over everything else, not because they are His own, but because they constitute the greatest good.

All beings, when compared with God, are less than nothing and are pure vanity. God's capacity for enjoying happiness or enduring pain is infinite, not only in duration, but also in degree. All the happiness or misery of creatures, though it might be endless in duration, would only be finite in degree. But God's happiness is both endless in duration and infinite in degree. Is it not right, therefore, that all His creatures should value His happiness and glory infinitely above their own? Is it not right that He should do this, not because it is His own happiness, but because it is an infinitely greater good?

Does not the eternal law of right demand that God should regard His own happiness according to its real value? Does He have any right to prefer the happiness of His creatures above His own? Does not justice require that He regard everything in the universe according to its relative importance, and should He not regard His own happiness and glory infinitely above all else? If He did not require all His intelligent creatures to do the same, would it not be an obvious departure from the immutable principles of right? Therefore, to have a supreme regard for your own happiness, to value it, and to desire it more than you do the happiness and glory of God, is to trample upon the eternal principles of justice that God is bound to maintain. It is to array yourself in the attitude of open and outrageous war against God, against the universe, against heaven, against the principles of your own nature, and against whatever is right, lovely, and good. (See Philippians 4:8.)

The Usefulness of Benevolence

Look at the usefulness of benevolence. The human mind is so constituted that benevolence is the source of its happiness, and malevolence the source of its misery. God's happiness consists in His benevolence. Wherever unmingled benevolence is, there is peace. If perfect benevolence reigned throughout the universe, universal happiness would be the inevitable result. The happiness of heaven is perfect, because benevolence there is perfect.

Perfect benevolence toward God and man would at once give us a share in all the happiness of earth and heaven. If we desire the happiness of others, their happiness will increase our own, according to the strength of our desire. If we desire their welfare as much as we do our own, we are made happy as they are made happy. Nothing but selfishness prevents our tasting the cup of every man's happiness and sharing equally with him in all his joys.

If we supremely desire the happiness and glory of God, our supreme joy will be found in the fact that He is infinitely and immutably happy and glorious, that He will glorify Himself, and that *"the whole earth is full of His glory"* (Isaiah 6:3). It will be to us a never failing source of pure, high, and holy blessedness. And when we look upon others and see all the wickedness of earth, we will see only the legitimate results of selfishness. Selfishness is the discord of the soul: it is the dissonance of hell's eternal anguish. Benevolence, on the other hand, is the melody of the soul. In its exercise, all the mental powers are harmonized and begin to breathe the sweetness of heaven's charming symphonies. To be happy, then, you must be benevolent.

Selfishness, you see, is neither reasonable nor profitable. Its very nature is at war with happiness. It renders you odious to God, the abhorrence of heaven, the contempt of hell. It buries your good name, your ultimate self-esteem, your present and future happiness, in one common grave, beyond the hope of resurrection, unless you turn, renounce your selfishness, and obey the law of God.

Why God Should Govern the Universe

Fifth, consider the reasons why God should govern the universe. Perhaps, in words or in theory, you have never denied His right to govern, yet in practice you have always denied it. Your having never obeyed Him is the strongest possible declaration of your denial of His right to govern you. The language of your conduct has been, "Who is Jehovah, that I should obey Him? I do not know Him, nor will I obey His voice." (See Exodus 5:2.) But have you duly considered His claims upon your obedience? If you have never attended to this, it is not surprising that you have refused obedience. The foundation of God's right to govern the universe is made up of the following three considerations:

A. Consider His moral character. His benevolence is infinite. Were He a malevolent being with malevolent laws, He could have no right to govern. Instead of being obligated to love and obey Him, it would be our duty to hate and disobey Him. But His benevolence renders Him worthy of our love and obedience. His benevolence alone, however, cannot give Him the right to govern the universe. His natural attributes must also qualify Him to be the Supreme Ruler of all worlds. A glance at His natural attributes will show that He is indeed worthy to govern. He also has infinite knowledge, so that His benevolence will always be wisely exercised.

B. He has infinite power. However benevolent He might be, if he lacked either knowledge to direct or power to execute His benevolent desires, He would not be fit to govern.

C. He is omnipresent, so that nothing benevolent is lacking in His administration. He is immortal and unchangeable. If He could cease to exist, or if He were subject to change, these would be fundamental defects in His nature as Supreme Ruler of the universe.

Yet neither His moral nor His natural attributes are sufficient ground for His assuming the reins of government. For however good He may be, these are no basis for His taking upon Himself the office of Supreme Ruler, without regard for the choice of other beings. But He is also the Creator, who holds by the highest possible tenure the entire universe as His own. Thus He is not only infinitely well equipped to govern, but by Creation also has the absolute and inalienable right to govern. He not only has this right, but it is His duty to govern. He can never yield this office or throw aside this responsibility.

The Reasonableness of God's Requirements

Sixth, consider the reasonableness of God's requirements. The laws of God do not have their foundation in His arbitrary will, but in the rightness of things. To love God and one's neighbor is not our duty simply because God requires it, but it is our duty because it is right in itself. God is therefore not at liberty to dispense with our obedience if He so desires. He cannot good-naturedly humor His creatures and let them have their own way—let them run into sin and rebellion, and then let them go unpunished. He is solemnly bound by the rules of His own government. Therefore, if you go on in sin, it will not be His option, on Judgment Day, to punish you or not. The laws of His empire are fixed, eternal principles that He can no more violate, without sin, than any of His creatures can. If you persevere in sin, therefore, do not hope to *"escape the damnation of hell"* (Matthew 23:33 KJV).

But perhaps, like many others, you have made this excuse for your rebellion: that God desires you to sin. You say, "God could prevent sin if He wanted to; and because He does not, He must prefer the existence of sin over its nonexistence, and rebellion over holiness." Disregarding what the Bible says about this subject, you have only to look into God's law to see that He has done everything possible to prevent the existence of sin. The sanctions of His law are absolutely infinite; in them He has embodied and held forth the highest possible reasons to obey. His law is moral, not physical; it is a government of persuasion, not of force.

It is futile to talk of God's omnipotence preventing sin. If infinite reasons to avoid sin will not prevent sin, then it cannot be prevented under any moral government. Physical power cannot administer moral laws. To govern the mind is not the same as to govern matter. If these were the same, then it would indeed be just, from the physical omnipotence of God and from the existence of sin, to infer that God prefers the existence of sin over holiness. But the mind must be governed by a moral power, not a physical one.

Because the reasons to obey God are infinite, He might very well challenge the universe and inquire, "*What more could have been done to My vineyard that I have not done in it?*" (Isaiah 5:4). And will you, in the face of all these considerations, continue your rebellion? When you are required to turn, will you profanely reply, "If God is almighty, why does He not turn me?" O sinner, why provoke your Maker? "[Your] *judgment has not been idle, and* [your] *destruction does not slumber*" (2 Peter 2:3).

The Atonement

Seventh, consider the Atonement. When the law was broken and all mankind was exposed to its fearful penalty, justice to the universe and mercy to sinners were immediately displayed in the Atonement. If God had made a universal offer of pardon, without regard to public justice, He would have virtually repealed His own law. But He could not forgive and set aside the execution without somehow securing a reverence for and obedience to the law. His compassion for man and His regard for the law were so great that, in order to gratify His desire to pardon man, God was willing to suffer in the person of His Son as a substitute for the law's penalty. This was the greatest exhibition of self-denial that ever was made in the universe. The Father gave His only begotten and well-beloved Son; the Son veiled the glories of His uncreated Godhead, and He "*became obedient to the point of death, even the death of the cross*" (Philippians 2:8), so that we might never die.

Now, if you are an impenitent sinner, you have never, in a single instance, obeyed your Maker. Every breath that you have breathed, every pulse of your heart, has only added to the number of your crimes. You have breathed out your poisonous breath in rebellion against the eternal God. How should God feel toward you? You have set your unsanctified feet upon the principles of eternal righteousness; you have lifted up your hands, filled with poisoned weapons, against the throne of the Almighty; you have regarded the authority of God and the rights of man as nothing. You have spurned every principle of right, of love, and of rational happiness. You are the enemy of God, the foe of man, a child of the Devil, and in league with hell. Why, then, should God not hate you with all His heart?

But in the midst of your rebellion, behold the longsuffering of God. With great patience He has borne with all your wickedness! You have done all this, and He has remained silent. Do you dare to think that He will never reprove you?

The Conditions of the Gospel

Eighth, consider the required conditions of the Gospel: repentance and faith. To repent is to hate and renounce your sin. This requirement is not arbitrary on the part of God. Can He forgive you but allow you to persevere in sin? No; this would be to give up His law and to publicly confess Himself wrong and you right, to renounce the stand He has taken, to condemn Himself and justify you. This would be a proclamation that sin is right and holiness is wrong. Moreover, to forgive you and leave you in your sin would render your happiness impossible. You might as well say a man is healthy who is dying of cancer.

Faith, like repentance, is also not an arbitrary requirement of God. God has no means of getting you to heaven unless you believe His Word and walk in the path He points out to you. If you will not believe what He tells you of heaven and hell, of the way to avoid the one and gain the other, your salvation is impossible. You cannot find heaven at the end of the road that leads to hell, nor hell at the end of the road that leads to heaven, and nothing but faith in what God tells you can influence you to take the path that leads to heaven.

And now, sinner, do you know of any reason why the penalty of His law should not be executed upon you? You have never cared for God, so why should He be under obligation to care for you? You have never obeyed Him, so what good do you deserve from His hands? You have always disobeyed Him, so what evil do you not deserve? You have broken His law, despised His grace, and grieved His Spirit. The tendency of your selfish conduct has been to ruin the universe, to dethrone God, to build up the throne and establish the dominion of Satan, to damn yourself and all mankind. This you cannot deny. Let conscience pass its sentence upon you. Do you not, even now, hear it cry out in the deep recesses of your soul, "Guilty, guilty, and worthy of eternal death"?

What is the conclusion to all these considerations? In this chapter, you have seen the reasonableness of benevolence and the hatefulness of selfishness; the right and the duty of God to govern you, and your obligation to obey; the reasonableness and usefulness of virtue and the unreasonableness, guilt, and evil of sin. What is your present duty? Is it right, is it reasonable, is it expedient to pursue your selfish course any longer? Is it not best, right, and honorable to turn and obey your Maker?

The Consequences of Your Present Course

Look at the consequences of your present course of action—consequences that affect yourself, your friends, the church, and even the world. Will you continue to throw all your influence, your time and talents, your body and soul, into the scale of selfishness? Will all your

influence continue to be upon the wrong side, to increase the wickedness and misery of earth, to gratify the Devil and grieve the Son of
God? Sinner, if you go to hell, you ought to be willing to go alone;
having company will only increase your pain. Should you not, then,
instantly throw all your influence into the other side of the balance,
to roll back the tide of death and save your fellowmen from hell? Do
you see the reasonableness of this? Do not stop to look at your emotions or your present state of mind, but cease your rebellion, throw
down your weapons, and enlist in the service of Jesus Christ.

Jesus has come to destroy the works of the Devil, to demol-
ish his empire, and to reestablish the government of God in the
hearts of men. Do you want Him to govern the world? If you were
allowed to vote, would you elect Him as Supreme Governor of the
world? Will you obey Him?

I can imagine your crying out, "Oh, I am such a great sinner! How
can there be any mercy for me?" That is not the question. The question is not whether He will pardon you, but whether you will obey
Him. If He saw it was unwise to pardon you, if the circumstances of
His government required your damnation, you would not be as obligated to obey Him. The question for you to settle is whether you will
obey Him and leave the matter of your salvation for Him to settle.
He is infinitely wise, and as benevolent as He is wise. Therefore, you
ought cheerfully to submit your final destiny to Him, to make your
duty your highest goal, and obedience your constant aim.

The Atonement is full and perfect. You have the promise that,
if you submit to God's will, you will have eternal life. Do you see
what you ought to do? Are you willing to do it? *"Choose for yourselves this day whom you will serve"* (Joshua 24:15). To choose God
and His service, to prefer these over your own interests and everything else, is to change your heart. Have you done it? Do you still
ask, "How can I do it?" You might as well be asking, "How can
I walk down the street?" To walk down the street requires two

things: to be willing, and to put your body in motion. But here, in this case, no muscular power is needed. Only one thing is required, and that is a willing mind. Your consent is all that is needed. Be willing to do your duty, and do it, and the work is done.

Remarks

1. *You can see why many people complain that they cannot submit to God.* They do not consider what is necessary to lead them to submission. Many only consider their feelings and look steadily at the darkness of their own minds and the hardness of their own hearts. They are anxiously waiting for certain feelings to occur, which they suppose must precede conversion.

Others, instead of attending to the reasonableness of their Maker's claims, give their whole attention to their own danger and try to submit while they are only influenced by fear. This is acting under the influence of self-love. Under such influence, the mind may struggle until the Day of Judgment, and still the soul will not submit. It is the rightness of the duty, and not the danger that results from not performing it, that must influence the mind to act virtuously. Both hope and fear play an important part in leading the mind to make the necessary investigation, but neither is the focus of the mind's attention at the instant of submission. Anyone who does not understand what can lead him to a right decision will naturally complain that he does not know how to submit.

2. *You see that the Spirit of God operates in the conversion of men through their attention and conscience.* The Spirit gets and keeps the attention of the mind, and, through the influence of hope, fear, and conscience, conducts the sinner along the path of truth, until He has given the conscience the necessary information to exert its utmost power. Then, when the conscience gives forth its verdict, the will may respond.

3. *This is the experience of every Christian.* Every Christian knows that in this way the Spirit of God exerted His influence to change his heart. His errors and *"refuge[s] of lies"* (Isaiah 28:17) were swept away. He can tell you that his attention was arrested and then focused, that his conscience was enlightened, and that the subject was pressed upon his mind until he was induced to yield.

4. *You see how unwise it is, while pressing the sinner to submission, to divert his mind and turn his attention to the subject of the Spirit's influence.* While his attention is directed to that subject, his submission is impossible. He can only submit when his entire attention is directed to the reasons for submission. Every diversion of his attention only multiplies the obstacles in his way. No biblical account that calls upon sinners to repent directs their attention to the subject of divine influence. When Joshua assembled the people of Israel, laid their duty before them, and said, *"Choose for yourselves this day whom you will serve"* (Joshua 24:15), he did not remind them at the same time of their dependence upon the Spirit of God. Rather, he reminded them of the single point upon which they were to choose, until their choice was made. We find this to be the same on the Day of Pentecost (see Acts 2:37–40), in the case of the jailer (see Acts 16:25–32), and indeed in every other case where men are called to immediate repentance.

5. *You see why so many sermons are lost upon the souls of men.* The sinner's attention is not secured; or, if it is secured, it is often directed to irrelevant matters, and the subject is confused by extraneous considerations that have nothing to do with the sinner's immediate duty. Often the subject is not cleared up for him; or, if he understands it, he does not see its personal application to himself. Or, if he sees this, he is not made to feel the pressure of immediate obligation. The preaching that leaves this impression is infinitely worse than none.

6. *You can see that there are two classes of evidence of a change of heart.* One is those vivid emotions of love for God, repentance

of sin, and faith in Christ that often follow the change. These constitute happiness; they are most sought and usually the most depended upon, but they are not the most satisfactory. The heights of emotion are liable to deceive; because they cease to exist the moment they are examined, they can hardly be depended on as an evidence of inheriting the kingdom of God. The other kind of evidence is a habitual disposition to obey the requirements of God— an abiding preference of God's glory over everything else—that gives a right direction to all our conduct.

7. *The concept of self-examination is made clear by this subject.* Many people will set apart days of fasting and prayer and spend their time examining their minds, trying to catch a glimpse of their emotions. In this way, they will surely quench whatever right feeling they do have. Their past thoughts and feelings, their past actions and motives, may be the subject of present examination and attention; but whenever they make their present emotions or state of feeling the subject of attention, they cease to feel. If, then, you wish to examine your heart in regard to any object, bring that object before your mind, consider it intensely, and if there is any affinity between your state of mind and this object of attention, the fire of emotion will burn while you are thinking it over.

8. *From this subject, you perceive the error of those who suppose themselves to have much more religion than others merely because they have more religious feelings than others do.* So many people seem not to be influenced by principles, but are carried here and there by every gust of feeling. While they tell of their raptures, their loves, and their joys, they have so little regard for principles that some of their behavior begins to dishonor Christ. Others, who much less frequently reveal deep emotion, are influenced by a sacred regard for what is right. They have much more of the consistency of the Christian character, but perhaps complain of the absence of religious joy.

9. *From what has been said, it is obvious that, where sinners continue to neglect the means of grace, their case is hopeless.* Many people seem to think that if they are to be saved, they will be saved, and if they are to be lost, they will be lost. They consider religion as some mysterious thing that will only be implanted in their minds when it pleases a sovereign God. They pay attention to every other subject, and occupy their thoughts with everything that is calculated to banish religion from their minds, and still hope to be converted. This is as irrational as a man who continues to drink in hopes of becoming a sober man.

10. *From this subject, you see the importance of giving a convicted sinner right instruction.* Great care should be taken not to divert his mind from fundamental truths. His attention should be removed, if possible, from everything that is irrelevant, from everything that regards merely the circumstantials of religion, and brought to focus intensely upon the main question of unconditional submission to God.

11. *You see the necessity of addressing the feelings, hopes, and fears of men as a means of awakening them and securing their attention.* Very exciting means are often indispensable to awaken and secure sufficient attention to lead the way to conversion. When there are so many exciting topics to call the sinner's thoughts to worldly objects, we must ply him with the most moving considerations, in the most affectionate and earnest manner, or we will fail to interest him and get him thinking about the matter of salvation.

Many individuals seem averse to addressing the feelings of men on the subject of religion. They fear to arouse bad feelings, and consequently they generally arouse no feeling at all. They obviously overlook some of the most striking peculiarities of the mind. They strive to arouse the conscience, but fail because they do not get the person's attention. The attention will not ordinarily be secured unless the hopes and fears of men are addressed.

12. *We should carefully distinguish between an awakened and a convicted sinner.* Neglecting to distinguish between awakening and conviction has been the cause of many sad failures in securing sound conversions. Often, when sinners have been merely awakened, they have been treated as if they were convicted. Their spiritual guides have neglected to seize the opportunity to force home conviction upon them. The guides have called on sinners to submit before they understood the reasons for submission or the nature of the duty. Then, as might be expected, instead of truly performing it, they have imagined themselves willing to do so, until their awakenings have subsided and the chill apathy of death has settled down upon them.

When the sinner is thoroughly awakened, there is no need for creating further alarm. Indeed, in this situation, all further appeals to hope and fear are an embarrassment and a hindrance to the progress of the work. When the sinner's attention is thoroughly secured, one should attempt to seize the moment to fully enlighten his mind and lead him to a right understanding of his responsibilities and the claims of his Maker. Then, if there is any wavering of the attention, one should instantly appeal to the feelings in order to focus the sinner's thoughts. An anxious watchfulness should be constantly kept up to preserve attention and enlighten the mind as fast as possible. In this way, you will most effectively aid the operations of the Holy Spirit and secure the conversion of the sinner to God.

13. *You see that preaching terror alone is not calculated to bring about the conversion of sinners.* It is useful to awaken sinners, but, unless accompanied with instructions that enlighten, will seldom result in any good.

14. *You see why those who preach only to the hopes of men seldom, if ever, bring about their conversion.* One appeals to fear, and one appeals to hope, but neither reasons with the sinner concerning

temperance, righteousness, or the coming Judgment. These preachers often arouse much feeling and many tears, but when such appeals are left without the necessary, discriminating instruction in regard to the sinner's duty and the claims of his Maker, it will seldom result in a sound conversion.

15. *Lastly, from this subject, it will be seen that a deathbed is a poor place for repentance.* Many are expecting that if they neglect repentance until they come to their deathbeds, then they will repent and give their hearts to God. But how vain this hope is! In the weakness and exhaustion, the pain and confusion, the trembling and the anxiety of a deathbed, what opportunity or power is there for the mental intensity and focus that are needed to break the power of selfishness and change the entire current of the soul? To think is labor; to think intensely is exhausting labor, even to a healthy individual. But upon a deathbed, to look over the intricate accounts of life, to ponder and understand the soul's character and destiny, to hold the agonized mind in earnest and distressing contact with the great truths of revelation until the heart is melted and broken—rest assured, such a task is ordinarily, if not always, too great an effort for a dying man.

As a general rule, with only a few exceptions, people die just as they live. They cannot depend on the waverings, flickerings, and gleamings of the struggling mind while the body, in weakness and pain, is preparing to usher it into the presence of its Maker. Now is your time, in the wakefulness and strength of your powers, while the command to get yourself a new heart and a new spirit, and the reasons for the performance of this duty, lie fully before you. Now is the time, while the gate of heaven stands open, and mercy, with bleeding hands, beckons you to come. Now is the time, while the *"pearl of great price"* (Matthew 13:46) is offered for your acceptance. Seize the moment, and lay hold of eternal life.

Three

Traditions of the Elders

Thus you have made the commandment of God
of no effect by your tradition.
—Matthew 15:6

The government that God exercises over the universe of the mind is a moral government. It is not, of course, administered by direct physical power, compelling the mind to act in the same manner in which physical laws operate. God's moral government is made up of considerations and inducements designed to influence the minds of intelligent creatures to pursue a course that will promote the glory of God along with their own interests and the happiness of the universe. It lays down the exact course of duty. On the one hand, it offers all the blessedness of everlasting life, and on the other, it holds all the pains of everlasting death for its offenders. In this way, the clear light of truth is held before the sinner, and all the considerations that heaven, earth, and hell can present are meant to show him the exact course of obedience.

The law of God was clearly revealed to the Jews, but its power over their minds was often broken by a variety of oral traditions, handed down from one generation to another, that were considered to have equal authority with the written law. They were often the corrupt interpretations of the Jewish leaders, mere evasions of the spirit and meaning of the written law. We have an instance of this in the verses connected with the text verse.

The Jewish leaders had a tradition that it was unlawful to eat without first washing the hands. To this tradition, Christ's disciples

paid no regard. But because the oral traditions were highly vener-
ated by the multitudes, the scribes and Pharisees made the disciples' disregard of them an occasion for reproaching Christ. They
demanded of Him, *"Why do Your disciples transgress the tradition
of the elders?"* (Matthew 15:2). Christ rebuked them by answering,

> *Why do you also transgress the commandment of God because
> of your tradition? For God commanded, saying, "Honor
> your father and your mother"; and, "He who curses father
> or mother, let him be put to death." But you say, "Whoever
> says to his father or mother, 'Whatever profit you might have
> received from me is a gift to God'; then he need not honor his
> father or mother." Thus you have made the commandment of
> God of no effect by your tradition.*   (verses 3–6)

The commandment to honor one's father and mother included
the duty of providing for them if necessary. But the tradition of the
elders evaded this requirement and taught that if the child would
give his property to God, or if he dedicated it to religious purposes
and made no provision for his aged parents, he was blameless. By
this evasion, he nullified the requirement and dismissed the commandment of God.

The corrupt interpretations of the Jewish leaders had entirely
blinded the Jewish nation. Their carnal interpretation of the law,
their traditional explanations of the prophets and of the commandments of God, had so shaped and modified the views and
doctrines of the nation that the people entirely misunderstood the
nature and purpose of the Messiah's kingdom that they had so
long expected. The ceremonial Jewish laws, among other things,
were designed to point out the nature and design of the advent
of Christ. Still, the delusions of tradition had been so great, and
the people's expectations and views of what the Messiah would
be were so entirely erroneous, that when He came, they did not
know Him. His doctrine they considered as heresy, His claims to

the Messiahship as blasphemous. Hence, the nation rose up and rejected, persecuted, and murdered Him.

But after His resurrection and the pouring out of His Spirit on the Day of Pentecost, the traditions of the Jewish leaders were discarded by the Christian church. For a short time, the clear, unadulterated truth of God shone upon the world. Its power was instantly manifested. When separated from error, the truth, like the midday sun, poured its steady light in upon the darkness of the moral world. Converts to Christianity were multiplied as drops of the morning dew. Judaism gave way before it, the systems of pagan idolatry shrunk away before its glories, and earth caught and echoed back the hallelujahs of heaven.

But in the midst of this bright day, and while some of the inspired writers of Scripture were still alive, the corrupt philosophy of men began to introduce new traditions to break the power of truth. People began to interpret the Scriptures by corrupt and erroneous standards. The truth became obscured, its power was broken, its influence over the mind became less and less manifest, until a day of darkness came that spread the blanket of midnight over ages of the world's history and peopled hell with millions of individuals.

When it was seen that the Gospel had lost its power, instead of ascribing it to the fact that it had been corrupted, that human interpretations and traditions had broken its influence over the mind, men went on with their speculations. They quietly sat down and very learnedly endeavored to account for the fact that its glory had departed, by ascribing it to the mysterious sovereignty of God.

These corrupt traditions became multiplied to an enormous extent in the church, until such a thing as true conversion to God was hardly known. Many of these traditions were rejected by the reformers, and during the Reformation enough light broke in upon the world that many souls were brought to Christ. But still the effects were limited. The Reformation was only partial. The

Gospel still did not have its earlier effect. Something was obviously lacking if the glorious sun of righteousness still could not shine in its full strength through the Gospel.

The philosophy that still prevailed—and by which men were continually interpreting the Word of God—introduced confusion, contradiction, mystery, and absurdity into the Gospel. It has perplexed and confused the human mind, has clogged the chariot wheels of God's mercy, and in a great measure has set aside and destroyed the power of the commandment of God to the present day. All of this has been the work of Satan. It has always been Satan's policy, since the world began, to break the power of moral government over the mind and to introduce confusion, rebellion, and damnation into the universe of God.

I will now mention a few of the most apparent aims of the moral law, followed by some of the traditions and dogmas of men that have broken its power. The following are among the most obvious aims of this law.

The Aims of God's Moral Law

The moral law, first of all, exhibits the benevolence of God. A law is the expressed will of the lawgiver. It is a declaration of his attitude toward his subjects, embodying and holding forth his real sentiments and feelings concerning them. It is the exact portrait of his heart. We have only to look at the two great precepts that comprise the whole law and the prophets to learn that God is love. These two precepts command pure and perfect love: supreme love to God, and the same love for our fellowmen as we bear for ourselves. (See Matthew 22:37–39.) Universal obedience to this law would of course result in universal happiness. The makeup of the mind is such that benevolent affection is the source of happiness. Therefore, if the benevolence that the law requires were universally exercised, in the degree prescribed by the law, then universal goodwill, peace, and joy would fill the earth.

Second, the justice of God is also strongly exhibited in the moral law. It requires of man only the love for himself that is reasonable and right, and only a perfect regard for the welfare of his fellowmen, nothing more or less.

Another aim of the moral law is to convince men of sin. It does this by holding before their eyes a pure moral mirror that reflects the exact moral character of their every thought, word, and deed. It is the rule by which every action must be measured; it is God's standard by which every thought and feeling must be weighed.

The fourth aim is to promote humility. By comparing his life, thoughts, and feelings with this holy law, the sinner finds that all is wrong. On being weighed in this balance, he finds himself lacking. His self-complacency is destroyed, and his pride is humbled.

Next, the aim of the law is to destroy self-righteousness and to teach men their need of atonement and a Savior.

A further aim is to promote holiness and happiness among men, to show them the impossibility of being happy without being holy, and that without perfect holiness no man will see the Lord (Hebrews 12:14). It presses upon the hearts and consciences of men their obligation to universal and perfect benevolence, and it convicts them of sin in every instance in which they come short of it.

To sum up, the moral law is designed to declare the perfection of God and the total depravity of man. As it is a faithful portrait of the perfection of God's moral character on the one hand, so it is a faithful witness of the entire depravity of man on the other.

How Men Have Altered God's Law

But all these aims have been defeated in multitudes of instances by the traditions of men. Pharisees, both ancient and modern, have defeated these aims by virtually altering the precepts of moral law.

Outward Conformity Replaces
Inward Obedience

Some people have made obedience to consist of mere outward conformity to the law of God, regardless of the state of the heart. But God's law deals primarily with the heart. (See 1 Samuel 16:7.) It is the heart, or the intention with which an action is performed, of which the law takes notice. It gives no credit for the outward action unless it proceeds from a right intention. It must be love that gives existence to the action.

A man may pray, preach, give to the poor, read his Bible, or go to church. However, unless such actions are prompted by the love of God in the heart, they are not obedience, they are not virtue, for the law still thunders forth its claims: *"'You shall love the* LORD *your God with all your heart, with all your soul, with all your strength, and with all your mind,' and 'your neighbor as yourself'"* (Luke 10:27). No outward conduct, however pious or precise it may appear, is to be regarded as obedience to the law of God unless it flows from love.

Therefore, to make outward morality equivalent to obedience to this law is to defeat one of its principal aims. Instead of convicting of sin, it is now calculated to foster pride. Instead of exhibiting the true character of God, it holds Him forth merely as the promoter of cold, dry morality. Instead of making men humble, showing them their need of a Savior, it leads to self-complacency. It leads people to stumble at the doctrine of atonement, to misunderstand and reject the Gospel.

This is the view of the moral law that was so extensively embraced and promulgated by the Pharisees who led the Jewish nation to reject and crucify the Savior. They rejected the righteousness of God and went about to establish their own righteousness by an outward conformity to the law. It is the same with the Pharisees of the present day: they overlook the spirituality of God's law, and they think their cold, dry, outward morality is good in the sight of God and is what the law requires. They wrap the filthy garments of their own righteousness about them (see Isaiah 64:6), walk in the light of their own fires, warm themselves with sparks that they have kindled, and must lie down in sorrow. (See Isaiah 50:11.)

The Law Is Given a Negative Character

There are others who make the law of God of no effect by regarding it simply as having a negative character. They see it as something designed to prohibit the outbreaking of selfishness, rather than as something that requires the existence and practice of all benevolence and virtue. These people are content to regard the law simply as prohibitory. Then they spend all their time resisting the tide of corruption that flows from the deep fountain of the heart, instead of seeing the positive character of the law that requires every creature of God to devote all his powers to His service and to give himself up to doing good and promoting the interests of Christ's kingdom.

The religion of these corrupt individuals, of course, corresponds with their view of the law. It has only a negative character in their eyes. As long as they do nothing very bad, as long as they abstain from sins that would disgrace them in the eyes of men, they imagine themselves to be Christians. They are aware that they do not deny themselves, take up their crosses daily, and follow Christ (see Matthew 16:24); they know that they do not hold all their possessions as stewards—that they do not account their time and talents and all they have and are as belonging to Christ, to be used only for His glory. They know that they bring little or no good into the world, but they are content with doing nothing very bad.

Now, their idea that this is true religion, and that they are Christians, is founded upon their sad and fundamental mistake of the nature of the law of God. Right views of the law would anni-hilate these false hopes, would at once sweep away their *"refuge of lies"* (Isaiah 28:17) and bring them to a better acquaintance with God and with themselves. But it is obvious that much of what is called religion in the present age is this artificial, negative kind of piety that contents itself with doing nothing openly wrong, but does not do what is right. Ask such a person whether he is doing any good, and he will tell you, "No, not that I know of, but I am not doing anything bad, either." Thus the high claims of the law are set aside, its aims are perverted, and the hypocrite rests quietly in his sins.

The Jewish leaders, in the days of the apostles, had taught that men could be saved as long as they yielded a perfect outward conformity to the moral and ceremonial laws. In opposition to this, Paul taught that no man can be justified by the works of the law (Galatians 2:16), for two reasons: first, because all men have broken the law already; and second, because no subsequent obedi-ence, however perfect, can make restitution for past disobedience. All men are, therefore, already condemned by the law.

The atonement of Christ is the only ground of pardon for all men. Justification, in the New Testament, is synonymous with *pardon* and *acceptance*. Those who are saved are justified solely by faith in Christ, irrespective of any righteousness of their own. This idea was quickly perverted by people who maintained that if men are justified by faith alone without the works of the law, then good works are unnecessary, and faith in Christ is substi-tuted for obedience to the law of God. However, they overlooked the fact that without personal holiness, no man will see the Lord (Hebrews 12:14).

Multitudes of this type have existed in different ages of the world and in almost all parts of the church. They have not always been known by one particular name, but thousands have and still do manifest such strange beliefs and practices. You may recognize them as those who, when holiness of heart and life is strongly insisted on, complain that they are not being fed, that this is legalistic preaching, that it is not the Gospel, but that it is going back to the law. They misquote Scriptures while entertaining the futile idea that the Gospel is designed to repeal the moral law—not only to set aside the execution of its penalty in the case of believers in Christ, but also to discharge them from the obligation to obey the law. They settle down in their self-righteousness, render it impossible for either law or Gospel to sanctify them, and *"utterly perish in their own corruption"* (2 Peter 2:12).

It is true that many who profess faith in Christ do not live as holily and unblameably as if they expected to be saved by their works. Because they are less strict in life and indulge in more sin than if they were to be saved by the law, they turn the grace of God into licentiousness, making Christ the minister of sin. This perverts and abuses the Gospel. This is making the Gospel a license to sin and to break the law, and thus Christ is set forth as the apologist for sin, as saving those who make His Gospel into an encouragement for committing sins that they would not dare to commit if they had to depend upon their own obedience for justification.

The Penalty of the Law Is Denied

Again, others make void the law of God, and render it ineffective, by denying its penalty. The penalty of a law is the reason given by the lawgiver to induce obedience to the precept. The greater the penalty, the more weighty and influential are the reasons to obey. The less the penalty, the feebler and the more inoperative are the reasons. Destroy the penalty entirely, and you destroy all reasons for obedience, except what is contained in the nature of the precept. If the penalty is destroyed or taken away, it is no longer a law, for a precept without a penalty is only advice, which may be received or rejected at pleasure.

There are two kinds of people, both called Universalists, who hold traditions that nullify the power of moral government. The first maintain that men neither deserve nor receive any other punishment for sin than what they receive in this life. The latter believe that there will be a limited punishment in a future world; that when they have been punished according to their sins, they will be translated from hell to heaven. In this way, both sects agree on the assertion that all mankind will be saved.

There are also those who do not believe in hell, who entirely set aside the penalty of the law of God and regard the sufferings of this life as the natural and only evil consequences of sin to man. They reduce the penalty of moral law to something indefinable, the amount or duration of which they do not pretend to know. If it is not eternal, however, then it is only a finite punishment. However long it may be, it is still infinitely less than eternal, and it is less solemn, awful, impressive, commanding, and influential than an eternal penalty.

While Adam remained aware of the threatened penalty that was before him, he persevered in obedience; he stood like the stars and planets in their positions, balanced by the universal law of gravity. But as soon as his confidence was lost, he fell. Annihilate the law of gravity, and suns, moons, and planets, rushing from their orbits, would run lawless through the universe. Likewise, Adam, standing at the head of moral beings, stood fast while the deep conviction of the threatened penalty weighed upon his mind. But in an evil hour, the penalty was doubted and lost its influence; and like the sun rushing from its orbit and filling the universe with dismay and death, so he, as soon as the force of moral government was broken, rushed from the orbit of his obedience and filled the world with crimes, groans, and desolation.

The Universalists seem to desire to relieve the world of its anxieties, either by wholly denying or infinitely lessening the penalty of the law of God. But it is quite obvious that if they were to succeed in convincing people of these beliefs, they would completely annihilate the power of moral government. For if they could convince the world that God never threatened mankind with eternal death; that the sufferings of this world are all, or nearly all, that sin deserves; and that God never intended to punish anyone in a future world, would this promote obedience to the law of God? You might as well say that taking away the penalties of human laws is meant to secure obedience to them.

It is a well-known fact that even the penalty of death is not in all cases sufficient to prevent someone from committing murder. But is it believable, is it possible, that to do away with this penalty or to substitute a lesser punishment in its place would be sufficient to prevent the crime? Similarly, the penalty of eternal death does not always restrain people from sin. This infinite penalty does not have sufficient weight and power to counteract the selfishness of the human heart. Now, by what mad logic do some people arrive at the conclusion that to do away with the penalty of eternal death would have a tendency to promote obedience to God? It is futile to say that the excellence of the precepts of God is sufficient to secure obedience.

It is widely acknowledged that the happiness of virtue is of itself a great motivation to be virtuous, but this is certainly not enough to cause obedience to the law. If an infinite penalty does not sufficiently restrain the selfishness of the human heart, it is merely delirious babble to say that a finite one would do it. If the threatened pains of eternal death are not sufficient to hold back the overflowings of sin, will the simple consideration of the pains of this short life roll back the insurgent waves of rebellion against high heaven, and bring peace on earth and goodwill to men? It cannot be. This is not only contrary to fact, but also contrary to all wisdom.

We have before us a striking illustration of the deathblow given by Universalist ideas to the law of God. Their universal salvation never makes men holier and better, never convicts of sin and promotes revivals of religion, never engages men in prayer for the enlightening of the world and the salvation of immortal souls. Who has ever known the law of God, after it has been robbed of its penalty by the Universalists, to reform a drunkard, rebuke and reclaim a debauchee, or bring a high-handed sinner upon his knees and humble him as a little child?

A member of an orthodox church was a praying man; he attended church, was honest, virtuous, and apparently religious. But as time went on, he no longer attended the prayer meetings. Then he did not come to church on Sundays. When he was questioned, it was found that he neglected prayer with his family. On further search, it was found that he drank too much. He began to doubt whether there was an eternal hell, and he became a Universalist.

Now, who has ever seen the reverse of this: a Universalist who was a man of prayer, who attended Universalist prayer meetings, who tried to promote revivals among them, and who maintained a life of prayer, grow cold in his zeal, neglect the prayer meetings, stay away from the house of God, drink too much, embrace the idea of an eternal hell, and, on being excommunicated from the Universalists, join the orthodox church? No one has ever seen this occur. There is no tendency in Universalist ideas to reform mankind. This is plainly and abundantly established by facts. They may exhibit their traditions until the Day of Judgment, but far from promoting holiness among men, they will only open the floodgates of iniquity.

The Gospel Is Made Ineffective by Men

The Need for Holiness Is Ignored

Just as the traditions of men have nullified the law of God, so have they made the Gospel ineffective. Some have viewed the Gospel as merely a system of mercy, as offering a pardon for sin, irrespective of its purpose and tendency to make men holy. These people have talked and preached and prayed about the mercy of God; they have exhibited it as a remedy, without convincing the sinner of his disease; they have urged him to accept a pardon without convicting him of sin. Thus, by overlooking the holiness that the Gospel teaches and encourages and by exhibiting the pardon of the Gospel without requiring its duties, they have made the Gospel entirely ineffective. The Gospel, thus perverted, has no tendency to save mankind.

Overlooking the morality, mercy, and pardon of the Gospel can never save the souls of men. Justification without sanctification, forgiveness without holiness, is not only absurd, but salvation upon such conditions is impossible. These people, to be sure, stress the Atonement, admit the divinity of Jesus Christ, and exalt a dead faith even above obedience to the law of God. This class of people who profess faith are generally known by their great zeal for what they refer to as sound doctrine, and at the same time, they are reluctant to hear the self-denying duties of the Gospel. The doctrines of God's sovereignty, the perseverance of the saints, and similar doctrines are the only truths that they relish, but only a distorted and perverted view of these can feed them. They put much more stress on doctrine than on the practice that such doctrine is meant to produce. It is clear that they rest on the shadow and reject the substance. They are only hearers, but not doers of the Word, deceiving their own selves (see James 1:22), who will *"utterly perish in their own corruption"* (2 Peter 2:12).

There is another tradition that claims to recognize the morality of the Gospel but denies and nullifies its most motivating reasons for obedience. They preach good works but deny the power of faith and the atonement of the Son of God. But the power of the Gospel is as sadly marred here as in the other case; claiming to acknowledge its morality but denying its sanctions annihilates its power. The most motivating part of the Gospel is presented in the doctrine of atonement. Blot this out, and the Gospel has no power to save and reclaim.

The fact is, these parties are equally ignorant of the truth. The one denies the morality of God's law, and the other rejects the leading reasons for obedience to it. Thus the power of the blessed Gospel is destroyed, and the abettors of both these systems are still in their sins. That which acknowledges the morality of the law but rejects the Atonement is a system of self-righteousness. On the other hand, that which acknowledges the Atonement but overlooks the necessity of personal holiness turns the grace of God into licentiousness.

The Idea of Physical Depravity Is Promulgated

Others have nullified and broken the power of the Gospel by introducing traditions that have a direct tendency to prevent its being accepted. One of these is the doctrine of physical depravity. This tradition teaches that depravity is part of the human makeup, that it enters into the very substance of the human soul. It is thought to be something created in them, a natural appetite or craving for sin, like the appetite for food in the body.

Directly connected with this is the claim of some people that the sinner is no more able to embrace the Gospel than he is to create a world. Some of this class call on sinners to repent but are careful to tell them they cannot repent, call on them to believe but are sure to remind them that they are unable to believe. Thus, as some have humorously and truly said, they preach...

You can, and you can't.
You shall, and you shan't.
You will, and you won't.
You'll be damned if you don't.

Tacked on to this is the dogma of physical regeneration, another death-dealing tradition in the church. If human nature itself is depraved, if depravity is physical and is something created with the mind itself, then regeneration must be physical. It must remedy the defect in the body. It destroys the physical craving for sin and so alters the powers of moral choice that, to say the least, obedience and holiness are made possible.

Now, it is clear that no greater obstacles could be presented to the reception of the Gospel than are found in these three dogmas just named: physical depravity, consequent inability, and physical regeneration. They all lead inevitably to the exercise of a spirit of self-justification. A man has no need to blame himself for his depravity if it is part of his physical makeup. If it is something created in him and born with him, the obvious conclusion is that it is something for which he is not to blame. But if this view of depravity is true, he must and ought to justify himself. To repent of such depravity is impossible. A man might as well be called upon to repent of the color of his skin, of the color of his eyes, or for any of the bodily senses that he possesses.

It is also unjust, unreasonable, and impossible for a person to repent of his actual transgressions if his depravity is physical. If his transgressions are the natural results of a depraved and defective physical makeup, he is no more to blame for them than he would be for the effects of any disease with which he may be born. Now, how must we regard a Gospel that calls upon man to repent of physical depravity under pain of eternal death and, to complete the absurdity and the insult, informs him at the same time that he has no power to repent? This places salvation upon impossible conditions, insulting man's understanding and mocking his hopes. Is this the Gospel of the blessed God? Impossible!

The Doctrine of Irresistible Grace

The last tradition that I want to address is what is generally called irresistible grace. This doctrine maintains that sinners who are of the elect will be converted in spite of themselves. This is evidently related to the idea of physical regeneration; if that is true, this must also be true. But I truly believe that the idea of irresistible grace is one sure way to make a man content in his sins. He will be convinced that, no matter what he does, no matter how he may live, if he is to be converted, he will be saved in spite of himself. I cannot think of anything more calculated to break the power of the Gospel, and to strengthen the sinner in his rebellion until he sinks to the depths of hell.

I have already noted that the Gospel was corrupted early on. These corruptions have continued, in various degrees, to mingle themselves with the pure Gospel. And as more or less error has been mingled with the truth, the Gospel has been more or less successful. Its power depends on its purity.

Other Tendencies of Men's Traditions

In millions of instances, all these errant traditions have led men very consistently to justify themselves and to condemn God. They have been led to adopt "the waiting system." If a person is really unable to obey God, of what use are his efforts? While he believes himself unable, he will see no use in trying. That he must quietly wait for God to change his heart is the logical inference from such premises, and God alone is to blame for his continued impenitence.

Hence, when sinners have been called upon to repent and believe the Gospel, they have replied, "I am willing and waiting for God's time." In this way, instead of being told to get himself a new heart and a new spirit or else experience eternal death, the sinner has been told to pray and wait for sovereign grace to change his heart. Thus, when the sinner has felt ready to break down under the pressure of the requirement to repent and believe the Gospel, his conscience has been relieved, and the agonizing obligation to instant submission has been deferred. The sinner has found his pains removed, his obligation to present duty postponed; he has turned away and has sunk to the depths of hell.

And this is no surprise, for the requirement of God is set aside, and another rule of duty is substituted in its place. The requirement of the Gospel is, "Repent now, and believe, so that your soul may live." (See Isaiah 55:3.) It gives the sinner not a moment to wait; it presses upon him, with all the weight of Jehovah's authority, to submit to God. He feels hedged in, as with a wall of fire; he pants and struggles and is driven to extremity; he prays, but still the Gospel cries, "Repent and believe." He goes to church and reads his Bible, but his conscience finds no relief. The commandment comes thundering upon his ear: "Repent and believe the Gospel." Whatever he does or doesn't do, wherever he goes, the requirement still follows him and increases his distress.

But this is where he may insert the charming, soothing factor of inability. Someone tells him that God is sovereign, and therefore he cannot repent himself. He must not even think about taking the work out of God's hands. If he prays and waits long enough, he has every reason to hope that God will change his heart. "I feel so relieved," says the sinner. "I felt as if ten thousand voices were crying in my ears, 'Repent! Repent!' And the more I prayed, the guiltier I felt, for I had thought that God required nothing less than absolute, unconditional, and instantaneous submission. But your words are comforting. If all I have to do is to pray and wait for God's time, that will be easy." Thus the power of the Gospel is broken as another requirement is substituted for that of God, and the commandment that was about to crush the sinner in the dust is made ineffective by this tradition. The sinner breathes easier, feels relieved from the pressure of present obligation, and goes down to hell.

The more he multiplies his impenitent prayers, tears, and efforts, the more acceptable he thinks himself to be to God. Thus his fears gradually subside; his good opinion of himself increases; his delusions deepen. But his *"judgment has not been idle, and* [his] *destruction does not slumber"* (2 Peter 2:3). He is gradually but surely sinking into the slumber of a stifled conscience, of a hardened heart, and he is about to cry *"Peace and safety!"* (1 Thessalonians 5:3), until *"sudden destruction comes upon* [him]" (verse 3) that he cannot escape.

Universalism is another logical inference from these ideas. Assuming that people are physically depraved, unable to obey the Gospel, and forced to wait for a physical regeneration, one must either adopt the conclusion that God is an infinite tyrant or that everyone will be saved.

These traditions also have an obvious tendency to conduct the intellectual mind into the regions of infidelity. "What!" exclaims a man of intellect. "Am I to believe that a book containing such absurdities as these is from God? Must I believe that God has made men sinners incapable of serving Him? Has He suspended their salvation upon impossible conditions, made it indispensable that they should have a physical regeneration, and then damned them for being sinners and for not complying with these impossible conditions? Monstrous! Blasphemous! Who can believe this?" Thus, having neither inclination nor time for examining the Bible for himself, and hearing incessant changes regarding these dogmas, he becomes disgusted and very naturally concludes that if these are the doctrines of the Bible, its religion is but a dream.

These ideas have often produced the most dreadful rebellion against God. Sinners, supposing these to be true, and supposing that God would damn them if they did not repent even though they were unable to, have been led in many instances to curse Him to His face. Didn't He make them sinners?

Undoubtedly, millions of people who are now groaning in hell might have been saved if it were not for these traditions of the elders that have made void the commandment of God. The purpose of the Gospel is to bring men to immediate repentance. It lays upon them no lesser requirement. It never calls upon them to do anything less than to repent and obey the Gospel. But many people, believing that sinners are unable to do this, have told them to do something else to earn their salvation—something that God never required. In doing so, they have put off repentance and lost their souls.

Remarks

1. *You see from this subject why some people deny total depravity* (in contrast to physical depravity; I will discuss total depravity in detail in the next two chapters). There are two main reasons for this. The first is based on people's inattention to the spirituality of God's law. They confine their attention to the Ten Commandments and consider them as something designed merely to limit obvious sins. But they overlook the absolute, positive perfection in thought, word, and deed that the law of God requires, and another rule of conduct is put in the place of the law of God. Thus, when comparing themselves with a false standard, they of course mistake their own character. Instead of closely weighing their thoughts and inclinations by God's standard of measurement, instead of bringing their hearts and souls entirely under the clear blaze of the law of God, they weigh themselves in the corrupt scale of their own ideas and theories and sink down to death.

Another reason why men deny total depravity is that they cannot see how the physical powers of their minds can be sinful, nor how a God of justice could make men with a totally depraved nature. Nor can I. If this is what is meant by depravity, I not only deny total depravity, but in this view of it, all depravity.

2. *You see why some people see no need for an atonement of sin.* They have entirely misunderstood the nature of God's law. This

was why the scribes and Pharisees seemed to have had the wrong idea of the necessity of an atonement. Their system was all self-righteousness. Therefore, they thought the announcement of the deity of Jesus Christ and the doctrine of His atonement were blasphemous.

3. *You see from this subject why the doctrines of grace lead to a pure morality.* The reason is that some people have right views of the spirituality of God's law, and they understand the necessary conditions of the Gospel to be repentance and faith. They regard God's law, in all its spirituality, as the rule of their lives. They focus their attention on this, as upon a pure mirror; in this, they see their exact moral image. This leads them to be watchful, to pray, and to walk with God. And while the purity of the law's precepts annihilates every hope of being saved by their own works, they see that, until they are perfectly conformed to the fullness of its requirements, they never can be perfectly happy.

4. *You see why those who reject the doctrine of the Atonement, and who depend upon their own works and the general mercy of God for salvation, exhibit a false and deficient morality.* The fact is, their vague ideas of the spirituality of God's law lie at the foundation of their rejecting the doctrine of the Atonement, and as their view of the rule of duty is defective, their morality is similarly defective.

5. *You see from this subject why some who profess religion, when they are urged to live holy lives, when their sins are pointed out and they are required to obey the law of God, cry out, "This is not the Gospel; this is preaching the law! Tell us of the mercy of God. We want to hear about Christ, not about the law."* The fact is, such individuals regard the Gospel simply as a system of pardon, and they overlook its great purpose of making them holy and bringing them back to perfect obedience of the law of God.

6. *From what has been said, we may understand why, for so many centuries, the Gospel has had so little influence over the minds of men.*

For centuries, so little of the real Gospel has been preached. It has been so mixed with the traditions of men—so much that is human, so much that is false, has been added to it—that its power has been broken. All the errors and false ideas that have clustered around the doctrine of physical depravity have served to shield the sinner from the arrows of the Almighty. Physical depravity, physical regeneration, the sinner's inability, and all the other errors have formed so many hiding places in which millions upon millions have been entrenched until the hail has swept away their *"refuge[s] of lies"* (Isaiah 28:17) and the waters of Almighty wrath have overflowed their hiding places.

7. *Multitudes have preached the substance of the Gospel, but the misfortune is that they added their own ideas to it.* They preached and boldly called men to repentance, but before they left the pulpit, they were sure to tell sinners that they had no power to obey. On the Day of Pentecost, the alarmed Jews cried out, "Sirs, what must we do to be saved?" (See Acts 2:37.) Suppose the apostles, instead of saying, "Repent, every one of you" (see verse 38), had said, "You can't repent; you are dependent upon the Spirit of God. Therefore, you must pray and wait for God's timing." If the multitude had believed them, not one of them would have been converted on the spot.

8. *The day of earth's redemption can never come until the traditions of the elders are done away with, until all these dogmas that are like hiding places for the enemies of God are rejected and not mingled with the Gospel of Christ.* When ministers of all denominations will see eye-to-eye, will dismiss all these human traditions that encumber the Gospel, will take the pure commandment of God and present it with an uncompromising spirit to the rebellious hearts of dying men; when they call upon sinners to instantly repent, and treat them as if they were expected to repent; when they live, work, pray, preach, and exhibit the true Gospel in all they say and do, then, and not till then, will the full power of God's moral government be felt on earth.

9. *These traditions of the elders are the primary sources of most of the fatal doctrinal errors of the present day.* Universalism, as I have already said, evidently originated in the theories of inability and physical depravity. Universalists have reasoned that, if men came into being with a depraved nature, physically and naturally inclined to all evil; if they are unable to obey God, then surely a God of justice cannot damn them. Now, this is a logical conclusion from their premises. For, if God made men physically incapable of obedience and then damned them for disobedience, this would be infinite tyranny and injustice. Upon this hypothesis, most modern Universalists are right in rejecting mercy from their system and in placing the salvation of men upon the ground of justice.

But take away the foundation, and the superstructure falls. Annihilate the idea of physical depravity and inability; show the sinner that his depravity is a thing of his own creation, that his wickedness is found in his voluntary selfishness and in the rejection of God and His commandments; show him that it is not for his nature, but for his conduct, that he is blamed, and you destroy the very foundation upon which his Universalism is built. You convince him of his sin.

10. *As I have said before, you see the foundation of modern infidelity in the doctrine of physical depravity and its related dogmas.* Intellectuals, hearing those doctrines so often reiterated from the pulpit, become disgusted when they hear a call to repentance followed by the idea that they cannot repent. When they hear the doctrine of the new birth darkened by words without knowledge, when everything is covered with mystery, they look upon it as ridiculous, absurd, and impossible. They turn away from such a loathsome exhibition of the new birth as something impossible for them to understand, and they conclude that it is all a dream.

11. *It is easy to see why revivals do not and cannot prevail more extensively than they do.* So many people obstinately stand by these

crippling errors and constantly try to maintain these traditions to the point where they paralyze the influence of most of the church. Many good men wonder whether they should reject these traditions or not; they are in that state of betweenness, so that they can heartily exhibit neither one thing nor the other. While these are the topics continually held before the mind, it cannot be expected that revivals should prevail.

It is true that great and powerful revivals have sometimes exhibited these views, but the preaching did not take effect while such views were exhibited. Consider the following parable. A lady who had been under conviction for a long time, had often asked her minister what she should do to be saved. Each time, he reminded her of her helplessness and her dependence upon God. He exhorted her to pray and to wait patiently for God to change her heart. Each Sunday, he would frequently call upon sinners to repent. But before he closed, he would be sure to caution them against depending upon their own strength and would solemnly remind them that they had no power of their own to repent and embrace the Gospel.

One day, when this agonized woman was present, he forgot his usual caution, and after pressing sinners to immediate repentance, sat down without the usual addition that they could not repent. Before the last hymn had ended, the Gospel had done its work in the woman's heart; and after the congregation was dismissed, she stood, weeping and waiting to speak with him. As soon as he came near enough, she exclaimed, "Mr. _____, why did you not tell me of this before?"

"Tell you of this before?" replied the astonished pastor. "I have declared it to you every Sunday."

"Yes," the woman replied, "but until now, you have always told me that I could not repent."

"I hope," said the pastor, "you have not repented in your own strength."

"No, not in my own, but in the strength of God I have repented, and I would have done it before if you had not told me that I could not."

This is the tendency of "cannotism." If people believe they cannot repent, they certainly will not repent. How can revivals prevail, how can the world be converted, while so many are vehemently contending for these traditions of the elders? These dogmas have been exalted as fundamental doctrines, and those who do not keep these traditions are thought to be heretics. Christ might very well turn upon them with the rebuke, *"You have made the commandment of God of no effect by your tradition."* When will the day arrive in which this false philosophy is given up? When will brotherly love and right views prevail? Only then will righteousness run down our streets, and salvation as an overflowing stream.

Four

Total Depravity: Part One

But I know you, that you do not have the love of God in you.
—John 5:42

These were the words of Jesus Christ on a certain occasion to those who claimed that they loved God. Using this verse, I hope in this chapter to establish the doctrine of total depravity. First, I will show what the doctrine of total depravity is not. Second, I will show what it is and will prove the doctrine according to its true definition.

What Total Depravity Is Not

First, the doctrine of total depravity does not mean that we lack the ability to obey God. We have all the powers that are needed to give perfect obedience to God. If there were any lack of ability in our nature, our responsibility would cease, and we could not be justly blamed for not doing what we had no power to do.

Second, total depravity does not mean that our moral powers are in a mutilated condition. None of our mental or physical powers are in a maimed or mutilated state. If they were, our obligation to obey would be diminished to the same degree that our powers were imperfect.

Third, total depravity does not consist in any physical pollution transmitted from Adam, or from our ancestors, to us. It is impossible for moral depravity to consist in physical pollution in the very substance of our beings. If such a depravity were possible, it would not be moral, but physical depravity, and we could not be blamed for it. It could not be a sinful depravity; it would be a disease, not a crime.

Fourth, total depravity does not imply that any being is sinful before he has exercised the powers of moral choice.

Fifth, by total depravity, I do not mean that there is any sin in human beings apart from actual transgression. In other words, there is no physical depravity that is the cause of actual transgression.

Sixth, total depravity is not a way of saying that our bodies or minds have the same tendency to sin as a serpent has to bite or a wolf has to devour sheep. In other words, there is no physical appetite or craving for sin implanted in the substance of the body or mind.

Seventh, the doctrine of total depravity does not mean that people are as bad as they would be under other circumstances. If they were placed under circumstances of less restraint or of greater temptation, they would undoubtedly be worse than they are.

When I say that people are totally depraved, some people interpret my statement to mean that people are as bad as they can be. To them, the word *total* signifies the highest possible degree of depravity. But certainly this is not the meaning of the word *total* here. The sum of three, two, and five is ten. This is not the highest possible number, but is the sum of three, two, and five. When used to describe depravity, *total* does not mean the highest possible degree of depravity, but simply that the whole character of the sinner is depraved, that there is no element of good in it. It is not that a person does and says the wickedest things he could say and do, but that whatever he does and says is sinful. *"Every intent of the thoughts of his heart was only evil continually"* (Genesis 6:5).

What Total Depravity Is

Total depravity does mean that impenitent sinners are universally destitute of love for God. The text verse says that sinners do not have the love of God in them. It would be easy to show that this truth pervades the Scriptures. However, because I am dealing with those whom I affirm to be totally depraved, I do not expect that a "thus saith the Lord" will settle the question for you and put it beyond debate.

You are unbelievers, and no matter how you assent to the truth of the Bible in general, I know that you have no real confidence in its doctrines in their detail. I might gain your assent, but not your heart, by proving to you the doctrine of total depravity from the Bible alone. This kind of evidence will not bring the subject home to you unless you are made to feel its truth. I might quote passages of Scripture as proof of this doctrine, and then throw upon you the responsibility of receiving or rejecting it. But let me present to you some of the other proofs within my reach. I will attempt to prove this doctrine by drawing on the experiences of you, my readers. Such a method will place this doctrine upon a foundation that cannot be opposed.

No Delight in Pleasing God

None of us understands exactly how the mind works, yet there are some workings of the mind that can be understood even by children. They are facts of such universal and frequent experience that we know with absolute certainty that such are the laws of the mind. For instance, by experience, we know that we take delight in pleasing the object of our affection. To love an individual is to desire his happiness. To promote his happiness is to gratify that desire. To please the object of our affection, then, is to please ourselves. It is not essential that we aim at gratifying ourselves, or at promoting our own happiness, in our efforts to please the object of our affection.

When we act virtuously, we are not thinking of pleasing ourselves. Even so, pleasing ourselves is the natural result of our virtue. This principle may be seen in all areas of life. The affectionate husband or wife has no higher enjoyment than when he or she is doing things that contribute to the other's happiness. The affectionate wife is never more cheerful than when she is doing those things that she knows will please her husband. Lovers and other dear friends are so diligent in their efforts to please the object of their affection. They are eager to anticipate each other's desires; they readily and joyfully engage in those things that they know will give pleasure to one whom they greatly love.

It is an absurd contradiction to say that you love an individual but have no delight in pleasing him. It is impossible to love an individual and not be gratified in promoting his happiness. To say that you love a person is the same as to say that you desire his happiness, and to say that you can desire his happiness without delighting in promoting it is the same as to say that to gratify virtuous desire is not happiness.

This principle holds true in religion, too. Every Christian knows that to do the will of God is more than his necessary food; it is his meat and drink. (See John 4:34.) Are you ever happier than when you are doing those things that you know will promote the honor and glory of God? Of course, your main goal when you obey and serve God is not to gratify yourself, but you find that you are never happier than when you are engaged in doing those things that please Him. You search His Word to know what will please Him, and when you know His will and engage heartily in the performance of it, you unintentionally promote your own happiness. To please God pleases yourself.

But what about the experience of every impenitent sinner? Because of the very makeup of your soul, you know that you love to please your friends. But no part of your happiness is found in pleasing God. You delight in pleasing your children and other objects of your most endeared affection, but, I ask your conscience, do you take delight in pleasing God? Do you study to know what will please Him? And when you have learned His will, do you find yourself inclined, readily and joyfully, to perform it? Sinner, is this your experience with religion? Do you love to please God? Have you made it your business? Is it your happiness?

In regard to the affairs of this world, everything you say or do is related to the object of your supreme affection. If your greatest love is for money, everything is loved or hated, desired or rejected, according to the relation it has to your love of money. If you can make money by it, you have pleasure in it. If it would prevent the acquisition of wealth, you are displeased with it. Similarly, if you have an earthly friend whom you greatly love, it is natural for you to inquire, in everything you say and do, how it will be received or looked upon by this object of your affection. All your conduct is modified, and all your pursuits are regulated, by this controlling and absorbing affection.

Now, sinner, I ask you again, do you view everything according to its relation to the will of God? If you see it will please Him, does it please you? If it is agreeable to His will, is it agreeable to your will? If it will promote His glory, do you desire it? If it will dishonor Him, do you reject and abhor it? If not, why do you pretend to love God? You would not believe that your children or your wife loved you unless you saw that they delighted to please you. Why, then, should you deceive yourself by supposing that you love God, when you know it is not your happiness to please Him?

No Love for the Companionship of God

Because of our human nature, we delight in the company and conversation of those whom we greatly love. To commune with them is sweet. To be alone with them, to confide in them, to share mutual affection, constitutes some of our sweetest and most sacred joys.

This principle is also true in religion. In all ages of the world, Christians have delighted to commune with God. They have sought His companionship, and they have loved the prayer closet, where they can be alone with Him. They are never happier than when they are alone in secret and holy communion with the blessed God. Sinner, is this your experience? Do you love to be alone with God? Do you delight to pray? Is it your most sacred, most endeared activity, to get alone and low upon your knees and pour out your heart in communion with your God? I do not ask you whether you pray, for this you may do out of a variety of motives, but why you pray. Is it because you love to pray? Because you love to be alone and commune with God? If you are an impenitent sinner, you know that you do not love the companionship of God.

No Sorrow at God's Disapproval

Again, we naturally prize the praise of one whom we love. We consider it of the greatest importance, and it is indispensable to our own happiness, to have the praise of the object of our supreme affection. Human nature is such that it is very painful to know that our conduct is disapproved of by our dearest friends. This is so in regard to our worldly friends, and it is so in regard to God. Nothing will wring a Christian's heart with more intolerable anguish than the conviction that his conduct merits the disapproval of God. The Christian may have, and often does have, the most painful emotions if he thinks he has earned the disapproval of God. He has offended God; he is ashamed and cannot look up; he feels as an affectionate child or wife would feel after having done what the parent or the husband highly disapproved of.

Now, sinner, in your experience, is this not true concerning him or her who is the object of your greatest affection? And is it true that you prize the approval of God above all things? Is it your focus? Is it your delight to gain His approval? Does knowing that you have done what He disapproves of wring your heart with anguish, apart from all fear that you will be punished? Do you feel the same emotions of sadness, shame, distress, and sorrow when you have merited the disapproval of God as you do when you have incurred the disapproval of your most beloved earthly friend? I appeal to your conscience, in the sight of God. Are you not aware that you do not supremely desire the approval of God?

No Consideration for God's Feelings

In all our conduct, we naturally consider the feelings of those whom we love the most. The affectionate spouse, parent, or child is careful not to wound the feelings of those who are loved. If one finds that the feelings of the loved one have been wounded, he has no rest until he has confessed, healed the wound, and been forgiven. This is true in religion, too. If you love God, you cannot think that you have wounded His feelings without also experiencing pain. You would not complain that you are unable to repent. The truth is, if you were in the habit of showing love to God, you could not help repenting any more than an affectionate wife could refrain from grief if she had wounded and grieved her husband.

No Delight in Thinking about God

Again, we naturally love to think of the object of our affection. Everyone knows how sweet it is to meditate and to dwell upon some absent object of our love. There is a kind of sacredness in those hours when, in the stillness of our bedrooms, or while taking a lonely walk, we dwell in silent but delightful musings upon the character of him or her whom we fondly love. These musings enkindle our affections into a flame. Picture a businessman who is both husband and father. When the bustle of the day is over, when the distractions and cares of business have passed away, his busy thoughts begin to dwell upon his absent wife and his children. His heart is all aglow, and tears of unutterable affection fill his eyes.

This is human nature, and these laws of human nature act with equal uniformity when God is the object of supreme affection. The lonely walk, the quiet bedroom, the hour of sacred time alone, are sweet to the Christian. He loves to think about God, to dwell upon His glories, to look into the mysteries of His love, to meditate upon His glorious character until his heart dissolves in love. Thus the psalmist said, "While I was musing, the fire burned" (Psalm 39:3).

Now, sinner, do you love to think about God? Do you delight to have God in all your thoughts? Do you seek solitude and quiet so that you may dwell upon Him without interruption? And when you meditate and pray, do you find a sweet, tender, and all-satisfying happiness in it? Do you have emotions of love for God that are as strong—no, that are vastly stronger—than those you exercise when thinking of your dearest earthly friend? I appeal to your own experience, and to your own conscience, in the sight of God.

No Delight in Talking about God

Just as we love to think about the object of our affection, so do we naturally delight in talking about the same. It gives us pleasure to speak out of the fullness of our hearts of one we love. Sometimes our affection is so cherished that we must conceal it, but even in those cases, a great affection is seldom cherished without being divulged to someone. But where there is no reason to hide it, it is natural to make the object of affection the subject of conversation.

This law is manifested in the same manner in religion. It is a well-known saying that "out of the abundance of the heart the mouth speaks" (Matthew 12:34). Think of a person whose heart is ardent with the love of God. If God is in all the person's thoughts, then God and the interest of His kingdom will be in all his words. If his heart is set upon God, his lips will speak of God. And if his circumstances require him to hold back or he cannot consistently talk about God, then he will naturally remain silent rather than talk.

Now, sinner, look at your own life. Do you love to talk about God? Is it delightful to you to speak of His character, His person, and His glory? I leave it with your conscience to decide.

No Pain at the Withdrawal of God's Presence

We are pained when separated from those we love. Everybody knows this is true regarding worldly friends, and it is true in a still higher sense regarding God. Every Christian knows that he cannot live or have the least enjoyment if he is far from God. If God hides His face, if the manifestations of His presence are withdrawn, the Christian becomes mournful, lonely, and sad in the midst of all the gaiety and enjoyment of the world around him. Sinner, do you know what it is to feel as much pain at the withdrawal of God's presence from you as you do when separated from your dearest earthly friend? Do you feel lonely in the midst of company, sad in the midst of gaiety, away from home in the midst of all your worldly friends, if God's presence is withdrawn from you?

No Love for the Friends of God

We naturally love the friends and avoid the enemies of the object of our affection. We feel attached to his friends for his sake. We love to converse with them, and we seek their company, because their views and feelings about our loved one correspond with our own. Politicians who are in favor of the same candidate are fond of each other's company. And individuals who differ widely in other respects enjoy each other's company if they have one common and absorbing object of affection and conversation. Thus, Christians love to associate with each other. They love other Christians because the other Christians love God. They delight

in their company and conversation because their views and sentiments agree with their own.

But do sinners love the friends of God? Do you love Christians
simply because they are Christians? Do you delight in their conversation and in their character because they love God? You may
love some of them for other reasons, and in spite of their religion,
but it is not for their religion that you love them.

Likewise, we naturally avoid the enemies of our friends. Will
a woman become good friends and spend much of her time with
those who are enemies of her husband? Does she select as her
friends those who speak against her husband or her children?
No, she naturally and instinctively avoids them. It is the same
with Christians; they naturally avoid the company of those who
abuse God, unless they mingle with them to warn and save them.
Meanwhile, sinners flock to their own and befriend more and more
enemies of the Almighty God.

No Grief When God Is Abused

We are grieved when our beloved friend is abused in our
presence. Suppose you are sitting with your wife in your house,
and an enemy comes in and begins to abuse you in her presence.
When he has heaped numberless vile epithets upon you, he looks
and sees that your wife is in tears. He asks, "What is wrong with
you, woman? Why are you reacting in that way?" What would you
think of such questions? Could you see no reasons why his abuse
of you distressed your wife? Would you not think it strange if he
did not understand the reason for her tears?

What if your wife showed no emotions of grief or indignation
when you were abused by an enemy? You would evidently think
she was pleased with it. What? A wife pleased to see her husband
abused? You would immediately think her a hypocrite and find it
hard to believe that she loved you.

Now, the same holds true where God is the object of affection. Suppose your wife is a Christian, and you disobey and abuse God in her presence. Will you wonder why she weeps and tries earnestly to reason with you? When God is abused in the presence of His friends, they immediately feel emotions of grief and indignation, and this is why the company of impenitent sinners is so disagreeable to a spiritual Christian. It is not because the Christian feels above you, sinner, but because your conduct is grievous to him. When Christians mingle with sinners, it is upon business or for the purpose of doing them good, not because Christians can have any delight in the sinners' impenitent characters or conversation while they are still the enemies of God.

I ask you, sinner, are you grieved by those who disobey God? Do you feel emotions of grief and indignation, as if your wife or dearest friends were abused in your presence? Does it pain you, even to agony, to hear men swear in the streets, to see them trample on God's holy commandments? Can you walk the streets and hear God's holy name profaned; see His Sabbath desecrated; witness hosts of impenitent sinners trampling, with unsanctified feet, upon His high and holy authority, and not be grieved? Then you are a hardened and shameless hypocrite if you pretend to love your Maker.

No Readiness to Believe What Favors Religion

We are naturally accepting and pleased if we hear anything good about someone we love. It is a well-known fact that it is comparatively easy to believe what we want to believe. Our feelings can cause us to believe even the slightest rumor, and some of us will believe what we want to believe almost against what we hear. If something seems to go along with what we want to hear, we tend not to question the validity of the testimony. We see this happen nearly every day.

This principle also holds true in religion. When Christians hear of a sinner's conversion or of a remarkable revival of religion or of anything else that glorifies God, they show a readiness to believe it because it accords with their desires. But do impenitent sinners show that they love God, that their hearts are set upon His glory and the interests of His kingdom, by manifesting a readiness to believe what they hear in favor of religion? Examine your conscience, dear reader.

No Regard for Promoting God's Kingdom

We love to see things being done that promote the interests and happiness of those we love. If we greatly love an individual, we delight in those who honor him and try to promote his interests. We are not very particular about how his happiness is promoted, as long as the attempt is successful. We most naturally embrace those means that promise the highest success. Politicians are very wise, industrious, and energetic in devising and executing means to elect their favorite candidates. You do not hear them stop and criticize any measure if it has a good chance of accomplishing their favorite goal.

So it is with Christians whose hearts are set upon promoting the glory and honor of God. They are on the alert, looking out for and devising new means of bringing about their goal. They are industrious and energetic in finding out new ways to bring about the salvation of the world. But do sinners show that they are interested in the glory of God? Are they planning and devising great things for Zion? Are they finding out new and more successful methods of promoting the glory of God and the salvation of men? Do you, sinner, rejoice when some new measure is introduced that has a tendency to promote this great work? Do you hail it as one of the means by which this great objective is to be accomplished?

No Difficulty Believing Evil of Religion

It is difficult for us to believe an evil report of one whom we love. Tell an affectionate wife about some disgraceful conduct of her husband, or tell a mother about the dissolute conduct of her only son. Will they be ready and willing to believe these reports? Do they believe you without question? No, they will carefully sift the testimony, criticize, and scrutinize; perhaps no weight of evidence will thoroughly convince them of the facts. Has there ever been a lawyer who has not seen the difficulty of convincing a juror against his will? If the juror strongly desires that the testimony of a witness should not be true, even a slight appearance of inconsistency will cause the juror to disbelieve the testimony.

This principle is the same in religion. Tell earnest Christians a story, whether true or false, that is dishonorable to God and injurious to the interests of His kingdom, and they will instantly ask by what authority you speak. They will carefully scrutinize the testimony. But do sinners show this unwillingness to believe evil reports of religion? If you hear an evil rumor about the family of a close friend of yours, if you hear that one of the sons had greatly disgraced his father, who was your most beloved friend, would a general story satisfy you? Would mere rumors be considered sufficient proof, so that you will believe it? No, you would ask for unquestionable authority, and even then, you would say, "I can hardly believe it!"

Now, sinner, when you hear a scandalous rumor about a deacon or minister or any other child of God, do you find yourself instantly resisting the report? Do you find yourself inclined to ask for further proof, to criticize the testimony, to weigh and scrutinize it until you dismiss the rumor as false and slanderous if you find discrepancy or absurdity in it? Do you feel indignation, and are your thoughts and feelings strongly repelled, when such a God-dishonoring rumor is circulating? When such stories are reported about Christians, do you feel as you would about slander that was uttered against your wife or your dearest earthly friend?

No Reluctance to Spread Evil Reports about Religion

Again, when we are compelled to believe an evil rumor about the object of our affection, we are careful not to give it unnecessary publicity. Does a mother go and announce everywhere the disgrace of her children? Does an affectionate wife declare to everyone she meets the disgrace of her beloved husband? No, no. She locks it up; she seals up her lips in silence and does not speak of the errors of those she loves. It is the same with Christians: when they are convinced beyond all doubt that something has dishonored God and religion, do they go and publicize it everywhere? No; unless they are compelled by conscience to give it utterance, it remains a secret in themselves.

So let me ask you, sinner, are you careful not to circulate what you know to be true, if it would be to the discredit of religion and the friends of God? Suppose you had seen a minister or some other child of God off his guard, and had witnessed his commission of some disgraceful sin. Would you lock it up as a secret and never breathe it forth, lest it should take wings and bring dishonor to God? If you hear an individual repeating something that is dishonorable to religion, does it distress you? Do you reprove him for it? Do you endeavor to hush the matter up, and beg him not to repeat it? I leave this question with your conscience.

No Hesitation to View Religion Unfavorably

We naturally try to give the most favorable interpretation to any event that might be injurious to the reputation or interests of a friend whom we love. If an event has occurred that allows various interpretations, we naturally interpret it in a manner that is most consistent with the honor and reputation of our friend. If a circumstance surrounding a beloved friend of ours allowed for two opposite interpretations—one that would disgrace him, and the other, not at all—we would, out of human nature, lean toward the interpretation that was in his favor. It is a law of the mind that charity, or love, *"believes all things, hopes all things, endures all things"* (1 Corinthians 13:7), and is always ready to believe the most favorable interpretation that is still within reason.

We see this occur in religion nearly every day. Christians tend to interpret events in a way that is most consistent with the honor of religion and of God. But do you witness this same disposition in sinners? Do you, sinners, find in yourselves a desire to construe every ambiguous occurrence in a way that is favorable to religion? If something is said by a professor of religion that turns out not to be true, do you naturally ascribe it to mistake or to a misunderstanding, and find yourself very unwilling to believe that he meant to lie?

No Distress When God Is Dishonored

When any of the friends of one whom we greatly love falls into any conduct that is dishonorable to the object of our affection, it distresses us, and we do our best to prevent a repetition of the event. If the son of our dearest friend were to commit a disgraceful crime and, in our presence, be guilty of things that were meant to dishonor his father, we would naturally desire to reclaim him. We would love and pity him for his father's sake, would feel grieved and distressed at the dishonor that this son was bringing upon his father, and would feel inclined to warn him and pray for him. Instead of going and trumpeting his failings everywhere, we would naturally want to protect his reputation for his father's sake, and do all that we honestly and consistently could to cover up his faults.

Now, sinner, how do you behave when you see Christians err and go astray? Do you feel distressed that they bring such dishonor upon God? Do you pity and love them for their heavenly Father's sake? Do you pray for them and warn them, trying your utmost to reclaim them? Examine your conscience. I will not bring a railing accusation against you, but let conscience rebuke you in the name of the Lord.

Remarks

1. *It is easy to see why impenitent sinners think that religion is something very gloomy; it is because they have no love for God.* What would you think of a woman who considered it a very gloomy business to be with her husband? She might complain that it is an irksome and disagreeable task to do those things that she knows will please him; she might consider it a burden to engage in the duties of a wife, and you would say this was unquestionable proof that she did not love her husband. So it is with sinners. When they picture religion as something gloomy, meant to rob them of all their joys, it is proof that they do not love God and that they have no delight in pleasing Him.

2. *You can see why sinners grow weary and complain of having too many religious meetings or that the meetings are too long.* What would you think if you were to hear an individual, who claimed to love you, complain of growing tired of being around you? Suppose he said, "Oh, the time does seem so long. I do wish this meeting with you were over." You would not and could not believe that his heart was greatly devoted to you. Likewise, when you hear sinners complaining that there are so many meetings and expressing a wish that they not be more than an hour in length, this is an index to their feelings. They do not love God; they have no delight in His service; it is a burden and a vexation to them to be called to spend a short time in His presence.

3. *You can see why many who claim to be religious prefer parties of pleasure over prayer meetings.* Prayer meetings are the most delightful parties to those who love God. But to those who do not

love Him, they are not a source of happiness. When such meetings are attended by these people, it is out of other motives than love for God. Whenever you see Christians showing more interest in worldly parties than in religious meetings, you may know that they are hypocrites.

4. *You can see that those who say they have always loved God are deceived.* Of course, there may be some instances in which people may have been converted at such a young age that they cannot remember the time when they did not love God. These instances are very rare, and I am certain that even some of these people who think they have always loved God are deceived. These are the people who have never had a change of heart; they feel toward God as they always did. If they had ever truly loved God when they first exercised this love, they would know that it was something new to them, and they could not possibly suppose that they had always loved Him.

5. *You see from this subject that impenitent sinners are often great hypocrites.* They profess to be very much opposed to hypocrisy and say that they like true religion. They desire to see people who are sincere in what they profess. They think true religion is a good thing and are very much in favor of it. They pretend to be very friendly toward God and say that they love Him. Now, in these claims, they are extreme hypocrites. Christ might say to them: *"But I know you, that you do not have the love of God in you"; "You are those who justify yourselves before men, but God knows your hearts"* (Luke 16:15); *"Serpents, brood of vipers! How can you escape the condemnation of hell?"* (Matthew 23:33).

6. *You see from this subject the obvious hypocrisy of those so-called Christians who unnecessarily publicize the faults of other Christians.* Some professing Christians act like infidels by speaking of the faults, real or supposed, of the children of God. They complain about the imprudences and errors of those whose characters are

closely associated with all the endeared interests of religion, and they often do this when no such thing is called for. And, to give these things even greater publicity, they sometimes publish them in the newspapers, all under the pretense of doing God a service and benefiting the cause of Christ.

There have been cases in which those who profess to be religious have entertained passengers on trains and in other public places by retelling slanderous stories of certain Christians. Vast prejudice has been created, and immense evils have resulted from this unchristian conduct of those who profess to love the blessed God. But it would be impossible for them to engage in this work of death, this mischief of hell, if they truly loved the cause of Christ. Publicizing everywhere the faults, real or supposed, of those who are identified with the dearest interests of Zion is absolute proof that they are hypocrites.

7. *Finally, with all these facts staring sinners in the face, how is it that they can suppose themselves to love God?* Nothing is more common than for impenitent sinners to affirm that they do love God, and yet nothing is more certain than that they do not love Him. What is the cause of this mistake?

First of all, they do not distinguish between an admiration of God's natural attributes, which they sometimes feel, and a love of His moral character. The omnipotence, omniscience, omnipresence, eternity, and wisdom of God are attributes that are meant to inspire awe and admiration in all intelligent beings, whether they are sinful or holy. But these attributes have no moral character. The Devil himself may be filled with awe and admiration when contemplating the displays of God's natural attributes, which are manifested throughout all creation.

Second, sinners mistake a selfish gratitude for love for God. A supremely selfish being may be grateful for favors bestowed upon himself, without any true regard for the character of the person who bestowed the blessing. Sometimes, when sinners escape death and some providence has worked on their behalf, they feel a kind of gratitude. Yet they might feel the same kind of gratitude to Satan as they do to God if he had bestowed the same favor upon them.

Third, sinners also make their own gods and fall in love with a god of their own creation. They imagine God to be such a being as they desire Him to be. They strip Him of His essential attributes and ascribe to Him a character that suits them. Then they fall in love with their imaginary god, walk by the light of their own fires, and surround themselves with sparks of their own kindling. (See Isaiah 50:11.) The Universalist, for example, creates a god for himself and thinks of him as a being who is perfectly suited to his tastes. Then, if you do not remind him of the essential attributes of justice and truth, he will talk and feel very piously. But if you present to him the true character of God, his heart immediately becomes like the troubled ocean when it cannot rest.

If sinners imagine that they love God already, it is not likely that they ever will love Him. Sinner, if you think that you love God already, you will never realize that you need a change of heart. If you really do love Him, you certainly do not need a new heart, unless you want a heart that does not love Him. By pretending that you love God, you deny the very foundation of the doctrine of the new birth.

Let me tell you, sinner, your delusion will soon be torn away. You cannot always deceive yourself with the thought that you love God. You are going rapidly to eternity. Even now, there might be only but a step between you and death. The moment you appear in the presence of your Maker and see the infinite difference between your character and His, your delusion will vanish forever. You pretend to love God while you know that you have no delight in His Word, worship, or service. Oh, what would heaven be to you when you cannot enjoy a prayer meeting for one hour? And what would you do in heaven, employed in God's service forever and ever? Would heaven be heaven to you? Would you feel at home? Would you be happy there? Not without the love of God in you. Get rid of this delusion, for *"most assuredly, I say to you, unless one is born again, he cannot see the kingdom of God"* (John 3:3).

Five

Total Depravity: Part Two

*The carnal mind is enmity against God; for it is not subject
to the law of God, nor indeed can be.*
—Romans 8:7

The law spoken of in the above verse is the moral law, or the law that requires men to love God with all their hearts, and their neighbors as themselves. Paul affirmed here that *"the carnal mind is enmity against God"* and for this reason *"is not subject to the law of God."* In other words, the carnal mind does not obey the law of God, nor can it obey this law while it continues to be *"enmity against God."* The apostle did not imply that a sinner cannot love God, but that a carnal mind cannot love God, for to say that a carnal mind can love God is the same as to say that hatred itself can be love.

In this chapter, I will show, first of all, what is not meant by the carnal mind; second, what the carnal mind does mean; third, that everyone who has not been born by the Spirit of God has a carnal mind; and, fourth, that this carnal mind is enmity against God.

What the Carnal Mind Is Not

When the Scriptures say that *"the carnal mind is enmity against God,"* this does not mean that any part of the actual substance of the mind or body hates God. There is nothing in the substance of the body or mind that is opposed to God. *"The carnal mind"* also does not mean that because of our human nature, we are opposed to God. None of our natural appetites or propensities are enmity against God.

Now, enmity may exist as a feeling that is known in the mind. However, *"the carnal mind"* does not mean that all unconverted men feel obvious emotions of hatred toward God. Enmity may exist in the mind as a settled aversion to God's character and government, leading us to treat God as an enemy without knowing that we feel hatred toward Him. Remember, emotions exist only when the objects that are meant to produce them are near. A principal reason why sinners do not more frequently exercise emotions of hatred toward God is that they seldom think about God. God is not in all their thoughts, and when they do think of Him, they do not think justly of Him or think of Him as He really is. Rather, they deceive themselves with false ideas and hide from themselves His real character, and so they cover up their hatred.

What the Carnal Mind Is

"The carnal mind is enmity against God." The proper translation of this text is, "The minding of the flesh is enmity against God." It is a voluntary state of mind. It is the state of supreme selfishness in which all men abide prior to their conversion to God. It is a state of mind into which they are probably not born, but into which they appear to fall very early after their birth. They turn the gratification of their appetites into the supreme object of their pursuit, and such becomes the law of their lives. They conform all their actions to this one goal that they have established for themselves, which is nothing but voluntary selfishness. A controlling and abiding preference of self-gratification rises above the commandments, authority, and glory of God.

It should be well understood and always remembered that *"the carnal mind,"* as the term was used by Paul, is not the mind itself, but is a voluntary action of the mind. In other words, it is not any part of the mind or body, but a choice or preference of the mind. It is a minding of the flesh. It is preferring self-gratification before obedience to God. The appetites of both body and mind are in themselves innocent, but making their gratification the supreme object of pursuit is enmity against God.

This is the direct opposite of the character and the requirements of God. God requires us to subordinate all our physical and mental desires to His glory, and to aim supremely at honoring and glorifying Him. We are called to love Him with all our hearts, to bring all our physical and mental powers under obedience to the law of love; and whatever we do, we should *"do all to the glory of God"* (1 Corinthians 10:31). Now, the carnal mind, or the minding of the flesh, is the direct opposite of this. It is pursuing the direct opposite of the requirements and character of God. It is a choice, a preference, that consists of a determination to gratify self and to make this the high and supreme object of pursuit.

All Are in This State

Prior to conversion, everyone is in this state of enmity against God. The Bible says that all human beings, by nature, possess one common heart or disposition. Our text verse does not say that the carnal minds of some men are enmity against God, but that *"the carnal mind is enmity against God."* In another place, God says, *"The wickedness of man was great in the earth, and...every intent of the thoughts of his heart* [it does not say men's *hearts*] *was only evil continually"* (Genesis 6:5). Another passage says, *"The heart of the sons of men is full of evil, and madness is in their heart while they live"* (Ecclesiastes 9:3 KJV).

Indeed, throughout the Bible, unconverted men are spoken of as having a common heart; and what the Bible asserts is a matter of fact. Go throughout the ranks of the human family, and present to them the claims of God and the Gospel of His Son. Require them to repent and give their hearts to God. With one consent, they will plead their inability to do so. Go to the learned and unlearned, the rich and the poor, the old and the young, male and female, slave and freeman, of every country and of every climate; not one of them can be persuaded to embrace the Gospel without the intervention of the Holy Spirit.

Now, how can this be true, unless the principle also holds true that, no matter how people may differ, whether in circumstances or personality, education or physical attributes, they all possess the same disposition in regard to Almighty God? They all, as if they are one, make excuses for not loving and obeying Him.

Enmity against God

This carnal mind, or minding of the flesh, is enmity against God. In the previous chapter, I attempted to prove that unconverted men do not love God. In fact, impenitent sinners hate God. This is evident in all their actions.

Pleasure in What Displeases God

Sinners manifest the greatest pleasure in sin; it is the element in which they live and move. They roll it as a sweet morsel under their tongues. (See Job 20:12.) They drink in iniquity like water. (See Job 15:16.) They even weary themselves to commit iniquity. (See Jeremiah 9:5.) They not only do these things themselves, but they also take pleasure in others who do them. (See Romans 1:32.) The very things that are the most displeasing to God are most pleasing to them. And the things that are the most pleasing to God are most displeasing to them. They love what God hates and hate what God loves. This proves that they are in a state of mind that is the direct opposite of the character and will of God. The whole tendency of their minds is the direct opposite of God's requirements and is enmity against Him.

Gratification When People Dishonor God

Impenitent sinners are also gratified when the professed friends of God forsake His cause and do anything to dishonor Him. They will speak of it with exultation. While Christians converse about it with sorrow, weep over it, and pray that God will wipe away the reproach, it will become the song of the drunkard, and wicked ones everywhere will laugh at it and rejoice over it.

Eagerness to Distort the Conduct of Christians

In their enmity against God, sinners are eager to magnify the faults of Christians and misinterpret all their right conduct. With a searching and malignant gaze, the eyes of unconverted men are fastened upon the professed friends of God. Sinners eagerly note their faults, magnify them, and are likely to ascribe every appearance of virtue in them to bigotry and hypocrisy. On the other hand, impenitent sinners often ascribe the most praiseworthy deeds of God's friends to the most unworthy motives. Their greatest acts of self-denial, those things in which they most humbly serve and most nearly resemble God, are so often misrepresented by sinners and made the very basis of opposition toward Christians. There is no possible cause for these things besides their enmity against God, for the people against whom this enmity is vented are often entire strangers to them—individuals against whom they can have no personal hostility. These Christians are hated to the degree that they resemble God, for the cause in which they are engaged, and because of the Master whom they serve.

Avoidance of Christians

We naturally shun the friends of our enemies. We naturally avoid the company of one whom we know to be particularly friendly to our enemy; his company and conversation are irksome to us. We see this same spirit manifested by impenitent sinners toward the friends of God. They avoid them, feel uneasy in their company. Their presence seems to impose restraints upon sinners, and they cannot abuse God with quite as much freedom when Christians are present. They are therefore glad to dispense with their company. You will sometimes see sinners who, when passing by a minister or someone they know to be a Christian, will avoid that person at all costs. The only principle that can account for this is that of enmity against God. These sinners probably have very little personal acquaintance with these ministers or individuals who claim to be religious, so sinners can only wish to avoid them on account of the cause in which they are engaged and the Master whom they serve.

Admiration for the Enemies of God

You will often hear impenitent sinners boasting of the talents and virtues of infidels and of those who make no claim of being religious. They boast of the excellent characters, high standing, and great influence of the leaders among the irreligious. At the same time, they depreciate the talents of those who are the friends of God. They often consider them as a sickly and bigoted people, and this consideration comes without any definite knowledge of the characters or the influence of the people of God. This is nothing else but the display of enmity against God and His cause.

Aversion to Thinking or Talking about God

We naturally hate to think of our enemies. Unless it is for the purpose of taking revenge or in some way gratifying our hatred, we naturally turn our thoughts away from an object that we hate. Similarly, sinners banish God from their thoughts. They are unwilling *"to retain God in their knowledge"* (Romans 1:28), and if at any time the thought of God is intruded upon them, they become uneasy and immediately divert their attention. If they are really convinced that they are sinners and are in danger of God's wrath, their selfish regard for their own happiness may perhaps lead them to think of God in order to devise some means of escaping His just indignation.

Just as we dislike to think about those we hate, we also dislike to talk about them, unless it is for the purpose of slandering them or pouring forth our malignant hostility against them. You often hear a man say of his enemy, "I do not wish to talk about him." Sinners are no exception to this principle; they are averse to talking about God. They seldom talk about Him, and when they do talk about Him, it is in a reserved manner that shows they have no pleasure in it. Indeed, such conversation is painful to them.

Irritation When Others Give Praise to God

We are naturally pained to hear our enemies praised. Suppose a group of Christians on a train begin to converse on their favorite topic, Jesus Christ. After an earnest conversation, they might ask impenitent sinners in the midst of them for an expression of their opinion. Or they might decide to conclude their conversation with prayer. How often the sinners are offended! Now, why do they consider this a disturbance? Why are they so displeased? Certainly they have no reason to fear that they or their families will be injured. If they loved the subject of religion, and if they loved God, would they not be pleased with the conversation? And is it not proof that they hate God and religion when they consider the kind introduction of the subject as an intrusion and an irritation?

Disturbance at the Prosperity of God's Kingdom

We are naturally disturbed and disbelieving when we hear of the prosperity of our enemies. If we hear that our enemies are gaining friends, popularity, property, or influence, it distresses us. We are inclined to disbelieve it. This principle is easily seen in religion. When a report of the prosperity of religion and of great revivals is circulated through a community, impenitent sinners will become uneasy and try to disprove it all. They will question the evidence and try to pour contempt upon the report and upon those who believe it. They do not believe that so many have been converted. "You will see," they say, "that the professed converts will all go back again and be worse than ever. The reports are greatly exaggerated, and if there are any Christians in these revivals, there are probably ten hypocrites to one Christian. Such facts speak for themselves." These people manifest a state of mind that cannot be mistaken: it is the boiling over of enmity against God.

Displeasure with the Zeal of Christians

We naturally hate efforts to promote the interests of our enemies. If any efforts are made to promote the interests of the kingdom of God, to honor and glorify Him, impenitent sinners are offended. They ridicule church meetings and speak evil of those who attend them. They denounce the zeal of believers as fanaticism and madness, saying that Christians deserve the disgust of all their neighbors for such things. People may get together for an all-night party, and impenitent sinners will not think it objectionable. In this way, the Devil may conduct meetings time and again, and sinners see no harm in it, no madness in all this.

People spend their time and money doing things that can ruin their souls, and yet sinners see no harm in this. But if Christians exercise one-tenth of this zeal in promoting the honor of God and the salvation of souls, it is talked about for months. Sinners may go to a party and stay nearly all night, but it is wrong, they say, for people to go to church meetings in the evening. Christians hold meetings and pray until ten o'clock at night! Abominable! Such things are spoken against in the newspapers. They are the subjects of condemnation in public places and wherever impenitent sinners are assembled.

Politicians may hold caucuses, post their flyers, print advertisements in the newspapers, appoint their committees, parade through the streets—all to bring men to the polls. Hundreds of thousands of dollars may be expended to carry an election, and all this is well enough. But if Christians even begin to serve God with such zeal and make similar efforts to build up His kingdom and save the souls of men, the wicked absolutely mob them and cry out that such efforts will ruin the nation. They label such proceedings as downright madness.

But is this because politics are so much more important than the salvation of souls? Is this because no effort is necessary to arouse a slumbering world and to bring sinners to act, think, and feel as they should about salvation? No, there is good reason for the highest possible degree of Christian effort, and sinners know it very well, but their enmity against God is so great that such efforts cannot be made without arousing all the hell there is within them.

Eagerness to Hear Slander about Christians

We easily believe an ill report about one whom we hate. If a man hears any evil of an enemy, he believes it on the slightest testimony. We frequently see this feature of the human heart in regard to religion. Sinners listen with eagerness to every false and slanderous report that may be circulated about the friends of God. It is surprising to see what absurd and ridiculous things they will believe. They manifest the most unequivocal desire to believe evil of those who profess friendship with God. It is amazing to see the enmity of their hearts manifesting itself to such a degree that often there is nothing too absurd, ridiculous, and contradictory for them to believe, as long as it has a tendency to cast contempt and ridicule upon the cause of God.

Readiness to Spread
Evil Rumors about Christians

We naturally love to publicize any evil report about our enemies. We desire to have others feel toward them as we do. It gratifies our malignant feelings to hear and to circulate those reports that are injurious to the enemy we hate. Suppose a man is talking to his neighbor and says, "Have you heard such and such a report of such an individual?"

"No, I have not," says the neighbor.

"Oh, I thought that you knew it, or I would not have said anything about it." So this man goes into the whole story and comments about all the circumstances of it as he goes along. He finally closes by saying, "I hope you will not mention this, but this is a true story." And soon he is conversing with another neighbor and tells him the same story as a great secret, hoping he will say nothing about it but thinking that the fact cannot be disputed. Everywhere he goes, he does the same thing. He is glad the event has happened, and he delights in proclaiming it.

We often witness this principle in action against God. If something takes place that is disgraceful among Christians and injurious to the interests of religion, sinners are always ready to give it publicity. They will talk about it, publish it in the magazines and newspapers, and send it in every direction upon the wings of the wind. If anyone becomes deranged in connection with a revival of religion, a great commotion is made about it. Thirty thousand citizens of the United States may die every year because of alcohol; homicide, suicide, and all manner of abominations may be the result of the consumption of alcohol, and yet the indignation of sinners is not aroused. But if a sensitive individual becomes deranged after considering his abominable crimes against his Maker, in connection with a revival or a church meeting, complaints are poured out upon the public ear.

A Mortal Hatred against God

Impenitent sinners not only hate God, but they also hate Him with a mortal hatred. That is, if it were in their power, they would destroy His very existence. There are probably very few sinners who are aware that they have this degree of enmity, and they may even be shocked at the assertion. Nevertheless, it is true. There are four reasons why they may not know that such is the state of their hearts.

First, it is probable that most of them have never dared to indulge any such feelings. Or they have never desired to destroy God because they have never thought it possible to destroy Him. There are many things that sinners have never wanted to do because they have never thought them possible. Did you ever want to be a king? Probably not, simply because you have never thought it possible.

Suppose that all the governments of this world were subject to you, and an opportunity arose for you to extend your dominion over the entire universe. Would you think it possible to subject God Himself to your control? Under such circumstances, would you be above making it your goal to exercise dominion over all the universe and over God Himself? Sinners, who would trust the best among you? You do not know your hearts if you suppose that, under such circumstances, there would be any limit to your ambition.

Second, sinners do not realize the greatness of their enmity against God because, as yet, God lets them go unpunished, and they do not believe that He will send them to hell for their sins. If God will let them have their own way, as long as He does not interfere to punish them for their sins or disturb them in their courses of iniquity, their enmity remains comparatively at rest. But who among them would not rise up and murder Him, if it were in their power, if He attempted to punish them for their sins? No, they would sooner wish Him in hell than allow Him to deal with them justly.

Third, it is evident that the enmity of sinners against God is mortal from the fact that they are in rebellion against Him and are in league with devils to oppose His government and to undermine His throne. Sinners do not obey Him. The whole weight of their influence and example is opposed to His government. They do everything that the situation allows in order to annihilate His authority and destroy His government. Rebellion is always aimed at the ruler, and it is impossible for sinners to be more absolutely in rebellion against God than they are.

Fourth, if you have any doubts as to whether sinners hate God with a mortal hatred, the question has already been tried. God has already put Himself as much in the power of men as was possible. The second person of the Godhead took human nature upon Himself and put Himself within the power of men. And what was the result? The people did not rest until they had murdered Him. You may say, "Oh, those were the Jews." This has always been the favorite plea of sinners. But are you of a different spirit?

The ancient Jews persecuted and murdered the prophets. The Jews of Christ's day claimed to honor the prophets and insisted that, if they had lived in the days of the prophets, they would not have persecuted them. But they persecuted and murdered Christ, and Christ Himself informed them that, by persecuting Him, they showed that they approved the deeds of their fathers. (See Acts 7:51–53.)

Sinner, you may not have originally murdered Christ, yet is it not a fact that you now refuse to obey Him as your rightful Ruler? Do you not support the authority of Satan, who has usurped the government of this world, by refusing to repent, by withholding your service and your heart from Jesus Christ? Do you not become a partaker in the crime of those who murdered Him? He required their obedience, and they arose and stained their hands in His blood. He requires your obedience, but you utterly refuse it and thereby show that you approve the deeds of the Jews. You also prove that, sooner than submit to His authority, you would murder Him again. In the eye of common law, this conduct makes you a partaker in their crime. In the eye of conscience, of reason, and of common sense; in the eye of God and in the judgment of heaven and earth and hell, you are guilty of the blood of Christ, and you prove you would dethrone and murder the Almighty if you could.

Sinners' Supreme Hatred toward God

Sinners also hate God supremely. That is, they hate Him more than anything and everything else. This should not shock you, as if it were a rash and extravagant assertion. It is the awful truth. Consider it this way: all other enmity can be overcome by kindness. The greatest enemy you have on earth may subdue your hatred by his kindness and win you over to become his friend. But why has all the kindness of God, infinitely greater than any human being has had in his power to show you, not overcome your hatred, but you still remain in rebellion against Him? Let me give you two evidences that sinners hate God supremely.

First, a mere change of circumstances in any other case of hatred will change the heart. There may be great enmity between two political opponents because their fathers were enemies. Therefore, they have always been enemies and have both believed and spoken only evil of each other. But suppose a political issue were to bring them both upon the same side, and they instantly became friends. They would dine together, attend political meetings together, defend each other's reputations, magnify each other's virtues, and cover up each other's vices. Their real feelings toward each other would have changed. All this would have been brought about merely by a change of circumstances, without any intervention by the Holy Spirit.

How is it, then, that your heart cannot be changed—after all the offers of heaven and all the threats of hell, after all the boundless love and compassion shown in God's giving His only begotten and well-beloved Son to die for you, after mercy has stooped from heaven with bleeding hands and has offered to save you while hell threatens to devour you—unless it is changed by the Holy Spirit?

Second, if men did not hate God supremely, they would instantly repent. Suppose that, when you are asleep in your house at midnight tonight, you are awaked by the cry of fire. You look around and find your dwelling wrapped in flames. You leap from your bed and find the floor under your feet just ready to give way. The roof over your head is beginning to collapse upon you with a crash. Your little ones awake and are shrieking and clinging to you. You see no way of escape. At this moment of unutterable anguish and despair, someone comes dashing through the flames with his hair and clothes on fire, seizes you with one hand, gathers his other long and strong arm around your little ones, and again rushes through the flames at the risk of his life. You are terrified.

In a few moments, you open your eyes in the street and find yourself in the arms of your deliverer. He is attempting to restore your fainting life. You look up and see that the scorched and smoky features of him who rescued you are those of a man whom you have supremely hated. He smiles in your face and says, "Do not be afraid. Your children are all alive; they are all standing around you."

Now, would you, could you, look coldly at him and say, "I still cannot repent that I have hated you so much, and I am not sorry for my sin against you." Could you say this? No, you would instantly wash his feet with your tears and wipe them with the hairs of your head. (See Luke 7:37–38.) This scene would change your heart in a moment, and the name of that man would be music in your ears ever after. If you heard him slandered or saw him abused, it would spark your grief and indignation.

And now, sinner, how can you complain that you cannot repent of your sins against God? Behold His lovingkindness and His tender mercy. How can you refrain from repentance? How can you help being dissolved in brokenhearted penitence at His blessed feet? Behold His bleeding hands! See His wounded side! Hear Him when He cries *"It is finished!"* (John 19:30) and dies for your sins. Sinner, are you made of stone? Has your heart been so hardened in the fires of hell that you do not repent? Surely nothing but deep enmity can stand against the reasons for repentance.

But perhaps you will say that you do not like to hear about hell and damnation, that you love mercy, and if ministers would present the love and mercy of God, and present God as a God of mercy, sinners would love Him. But this is all a mistake. Sinners are as much opposed to the mercy of God as they are to any of His attributes. This is a fact that is experienced every day. Can you not hear those cries of *"Crucify Him!"* (Mark 15:13)? God has revealed His mercy, yet all the world is against it. Jesus Christ has come to bring salvation, and the world is in an uproar to murder Him. Mercy is the very attribute of God against which mankind is arrayed.

For thousands of years, God has been unfolding and offering mercy. All the world's opposition to God and to religion is aimed particularly at His mercy. What is Christianity? What is the Bible? What are revivals of religion? They are just a few of the exhibitions of the mercy of the blessed God that have called forth so much of the opposition of earth and hell. When Justice ascends the throne, the slanderous mouths of sinners will be stopped. Justice will soon hush the tumult and loud opposition of sinners against their Maker. Every mouth will be stopped, and all the world will be found guilty before God.

But now, all earth is up in arms against the mercy of God. Why are you such a hypocrite as to pretend to love the mercy of God? If you love it, why do you not accept it? If you love a God of mercy, why has it not yet melted you down and subdued your heart? Sinner, do not speak proudly anymore. Do not boast that you love any attribute of God, for if you say you love Him while you remain impenitent, you are a liar, and the truth is not in you. (See 1 John 2:4.)

Remarks

1. *You see why the Universalists and other sinners are so disturbed by revivals of religion.* It is because God comes forth so obviously in the exercise of His mercy, and they cannot bear such an exhibition of God. It disturbs all the lurking enmity of their hearts. These professed friends of God and men are greatly offended as soon as God displays Himself and men become the recipients of His mercy.

2. *You see the importance of preaching, clearly and frequently, the enmity of sinners' hearts against God.* For ages, there has been a significant defect in declaring this most important subject. Ministers seem to have been afraid to charge men with being the enemies of God. Prior to my own conversion, I never heard anyone talk about this doctrine in a way that I understood it. Many ministers seem to have regarded total depravity as nothing more than the absence of love for God.

The church does not seem to have realized or believed that the carnal mind is absolute enmity against God. Although the Word of God teaches this truth abundantly, very few sinners have been made to see and believe it. In hundreds of instances, I have conversed with people who have listened to the preaching of the Gospel all their days, but who never understood this fundamental truth of the Gospel. It is a truth upon which is founded the necessity of the new birth and of the Spirit's influences. Without understanding and believing it, how are we to expect the world to be converted to God?

3. *From this subject, we see that, even if sinners were to swear that they hate God, it would not make it any more evident.* If all the men in the universe swore that the sun shines at noonday, it would not add a particle to the evidence that the sun shines. It is a simple fact, for which we can have no better evidence than our own senses. Likewise, it is fact that sinners are the enemies of God. They act it out in the midst of all men. They speak against revivals and those engaged in promoting them. They publicize the faults, real or supposed, of those who are the friends of God. They slander others and manifest their opposition to God in so many ways that their hypocrisy and enmity against God are perfectly obvious. This is as evident to me as the fact that they have an existence, and how it ever came to be questioned, or ever forgotten or overlooked, is a great mystery to me.

4. *Those who have not known, by their own experience, that they have been enemies of God, have not been converted or even convicted.* What have they repented of? Have they repented merely of their outward sins? This is impossible, unless they have understood and condemned the fountain of iniquity from which these abominations have proceeded. They have been the enemies of God from the beginning. Their minding of the flesh has itself been enmity against God. How can they talk of having repented when they have never so much as known what their chief guilt consists of? Impossible!

5. *Sinners who deny that they are the enemies of God are never likely to be converted until they confess their hatred.* Proverbs 28:13 says, "He who covers his sins will not prosper, but whoever confesses and forsakes them will have mercy." There are many people who confess that they are sinners but deny that they are the enemies of God. Thus they cover up the great amount of their sins; they acknowledge their outward acts of wickedness but deny the enmity from which they flow. While they do this, God will not forgive them.

6. *You see why sinners find it so hard to be religious.* The total difficulty lies in their unwillingness to give up their selfishness.

7. *It cannot be reasonably said that what I have written here amounts to any denial of moral depravity.* I have purposely denied physical depravity, but I have specifically promoted the idea of moral depravity, for which the sinner is to blame and of which he must repent entirely. Some people think that a denial of physical depravity is also a denial of all depravity. I have attempted to show that the cause of sin is not to be found in a sinful physical nature, but in a wrong choice, in which the sinner prefers self-gratification above the will of his Maker. This choice has become the settled preference of his soul and constitutes the deep fountain from which all the putrid waters of spiritual and eternal death flow.

Now, why is it called moral depravity? It certainly has no such relation to moral law as to deserve punishment. It is amazing that, in this century, it is heresy to call sin a transgression of the law and insist that it must be a voluntary act. Has it come to this? Are those who deny all moral depravity and charge God with all the sins of the world going to complain of heresy in those who maintain moral depravity but deny physical or constitutional depravity? What next? If it is heresy to say that sin is a transgression of the law, certainly the apostle Paul was confused in his doctrine.

8. *It should be clear that sinners must either be annihilated, converted, or forever lost.* With a mind that is enmity against God, it is impossible for them to be happy. Infidels have no cause to sneer at the doctrine of the new birth. If there were no Bible in the world, the doctrine of total depravity as I have shown it here would still be as abundantly obvious as any other fact. It cannot be denied that, unless men pass through the change of mind that the Bible refers to as the new birth, they must be annihilated or else damned for all eternity.

9. *Sinners are not almost Christians.* We sometimes hear people say that a particular impenitent sinner is almost a Christian. The truth is, the most moral impenitent sinner in the world is still much nearer a devil than a Christian. Perhaps you know a young lady who is an impenitent sinner. She only needs to die to be as much a devil as there is in hell. If God were to take His supporting hand from under her, the hatred of hell would immediately boil over in her. If God were to cease, even for a moment, to keep her lungs breathing, she would open her eyes in eternity, and if she dared, would curse Him to His face.

10. *It would be impossible for sinners to enjoy heaven if they were permitted to go there in their present state of mind.* If their unconverted souls were to burst forth into the presence of God to look around and behold His glories; if they could see "HOLINESS TO THE LORD" (Exodus 28:36) inscribed on everything around them; if they could listen to the song of praise, the song of "Holy, holy, holy, Lord God Almighty" (Revelation 4:8), their hatred would be so great that, if permitted, they would dive into the darkest cavern of hell to escape from the presence of the infinitely holy Lord God.

11. *While sinners remain in impenitence, they demonstrate no more obedience to God than the Devil does.* Their carnal mind "*is not subject to the law of God, nor indeed can be.*" Until the supreme preference of their minds is changed, until they have given up minding the flesh and begin to obey God, it is futile to talk of obedience. The first act of obedience that you ever will or can perform is to stop minding the flesh and give your heart to God.

12. *You see the wickedness and foolishness of parents who think their unconverted children are receptive to religion.* You cannot teach your children a greater heresy than that. I have often heard Christian parents say that their children are not enemies of religion. It is no wonder that such children are not converted under

such teaching! It is exactly the doctrine that the Devil wants you to teach them. If you only give your children the impression that they are already receptive toward religion, they will never know why they need a new heart. While under this delusion, they cannot be convicted, much less converted.

13. *You see the foolishness and the falsehood of saying that an impenitent sinner is a good-hearted man, when the fact is that his heart is enmity against God.*

14. *Lastly, you see how necessary it is that there should be a hell.* What can be done with these enemies of God if they die in their sins? Heaven is no place for them. A hell is deserved by sinners and is evidently needed for those who die hating God.

Now, sinner, you see your condition; you must be convinced of the truth of what I have said. Remember that your enmity is voluntary. It is of your own creation, and you have cherished and exercised it for a long time. Will you give it up? What has God done, that you should continue to hate Him? What is there in sin, that you should prefer it over God? Why will you indulge, for even a moment longer, this spirit of horrible rebellion and enmity against the blessed God? If you cleave to your enmity for a little longer, the knell of eternal death will toll over your damned soul, and all the corners of despair will echo with your groans.

Six

Why Sinners Hate God

They hated Me without a cause.
—John 15:25

These are the words of our Lord Jesus Christ. In the two previous chapters on total depravity, I have tried to prove that all impenitent sinners hate God more than everything else. But the solemn and important question yet remains: why do sinners hate God?

If sinners have a good reason for hating God, then they are not to blame for it. But if they have no good reason, or if they hate Him when they ought to love Him, then they have incurred great guilt by their enmity to God.

In this chapter, I hope to show, first, what are not the reasons for their hatred; second, what are the reasons for it; and, third, that they hate Him for the very reasons for which they ought to love Him.

What the Sinner's Hatred of God Is Not Caused By

A Physical Aversion to God

First, sinners do not hate God because He has made them that way or because they have a physical aversion to Him. The text verse affirms that sinners have hated God *"without a cause."* Of course, there is some reason why they hate Him, but it is not a good reason. There is a cause for their hatred, for every effect must have a cause, but there is no just cause. If God had created man in such a way that man was forced by physical necessity to hate his Maker, this would be not only a cause, but also a just cause for hating Him. But God has not incorporated into man's physical body an aversion to Himself; if He had, this would not only be a sufficient cause for the sinner's hating Him, but also a good reason why all other beings should hate Him.

A Hereditary Disposition to Hate Him

Second, the sinner's hatred of God is not caused by any hereditary disposition to hate Him. A disposition to hate God is itself hatred. Disposition is an action of the mind, not a part of the mind itself. It is therefore absurd to talk of a hereditary or transmitted disposition to love or hate God, or anything else. It is impossible for a voluntary state of mind to be transmitted from one generation to another.

Perhaps some of you think that *disposition* denotes a propensity—not an action that is an involuntary state of mind, but a quality or attribute that is part of the mind itself. Against this I argue that the sinner's hatred is not caused by any such attribute or property that is part of the mind and that in itself has a natural and necessary aversion to God.

A Just Cause in Human Nature

Third, there is no just cause in human nature for opposition to God. The nature of man is as it should be. Its powers are as God made them. He has made them in the best manner in which infinite power and goodness and wisdom could make them. They are perfectly adapted to the service of the Creator. If we survey the exquisite operation and delicate organization of the body, and all the properties, powers, and capabilities of the mind, we can find no just cause of complaint. On the other hand, we find infinite reason to love and adore the great Architect, and we exclaim with the psalmist, *"I am fearfully and wonderfully made"* (Psalm 139:14).

A Just Cause for Hating God's Government

Fourth, there is no just cause for the sinner's hatred of the government of God. Some people seem to take it for granted that the two governments that God exercises over the universe—moral and providential—might have been administered in a way that would have produced universal holiness throughout the universe. But this is an unwarranted and wicked assumption. The assumption is based upon an erroneous view of the nature of moral choice and of moral government.

There is no reason to doubt that God administers His government in such a way that will produce the highest and most healthful influence in favor of holiness. It is obvious that His moral laws are guarded by the highest possible sanctions, that everything has been done that the perfection of moral government could do to secure universal holiness in the world. So, beyond all reasonable doubt, His physical or providential government is administered in the wisest possible manner.

It is undoubtedly administered solely for the benefit of and in support of moral government. It is so arranged as to bring out and exert the highest moral influence that such a government is capable of exerting. Many sinners talk as if they supposed God might have administered His governments, both moral and providential, in a manner vastly more judicious and more highly calculated to secure perfection in the conduct of His subjects. They seem to think that, because God is almighty, He can therefore work any conceivable absurdity or contradiction and can make people perfect by exercising His physical omnipotence. They also think that the existence of sin in our world is proof that, overall, although on some accounts God is opposed to sin, He prefers its existence above holiness.

A Just Cause for Hating the Gospel's Requirements

Fifth, sinners have no just cause for their hatred of the requirements of the Gospel. If the conditions of salvation held forth in the Gospel were arbitrary, capricious, or unjust; if it were impossible to comply with them; if the terms of salvation were put so high that men would have no natural power to obey them and fulfill the conditions upon which their salvation hangs; if God commanded sinners to repent when they had no power to repent; if He required them to believe when they had no power to believe and threatened to send them to hell for not repenting and believing; in any of these cases, sinners would have just reason to hate God. But none of these things are true.

The conditions of the Gospel, far from being arbitrary, are indispensable to salvation. Far from being put too high to comply with them, they are brought down as low as they possibly can be without rendering the sinner's salvation impossible. Repentance and faith are indispensable to equip the soul for the enjoyment of heaven, and if God were to dispense with these conditions and agree that the sinner should remain in his sins, it would render the sinner's damnation certain.

Not only are the conditions of salvation necessary, but it is also easy to comply with them—much easier than to reject them. Our mental powers are as well suited to accept the Gospel as to reject it. The reasons to accept are infinitely greater than those to reject the offers of mercy. Indeed, the reasons to comply with the conditions of the Gospel are so weighty that sinners often find it difficult to resist them, and they are under the necessity of making almost ceaseless efforts to maintain themselves in impenitence and unbelief.

God's commandments are not grievous (1 John 5:3), impossible to be obeyed, or meant to produce misery when obeyed. On the contrary, His *"yoke is easy and [His] burden is light"* (Matthew 11:30). His commandments are easily obeyed, and obedience naturally results in happiness. If God had established a government in which the requirements were so high that it was extremely difficult to yield obedience to His laws; if the laws were so obscure and intricate and difficult to understand that an honest mind would be in great danger of mistaking the real meaning of His requirements; if His laws were arbitrary, unnecessary, and capricious; if they were guarded by unjust and cruel sanctions; if any of these things were true, sinners would have a just cause to hate God. But not one of them is true.

A Just Cause for Hating God's Character

Sixth, there is no just cause for hatred of anything that belongs to the character of God. To a mind that is reasonable and just, there is nothing hateful or repellant in the character of Jehovah. Rather, His character consists of every conceivable or possible excellence.

A Just Cause for Hating God's Conduct

Seventh, there is also no just cause for hatred of the conduct of God. There is no inconsistency between His conduct and what He claims. Some people seem to have an idea that God is a sly, cunning, hypocritical being who says one thing and means another. They think He claims to abhor sin yet conducts Himself and the affairs of His kingdom in such a way that purposefully produces sin. He commands men to keep His law, on pain of eternal death, but prefers that they should break it, after all. He commands all men to repent and believe the Gospel yet has made atonement only for the elect. While He requires men to repent, He has given them a nature that makes them unable to repent. He claims to greatly desire the salvation of all men, and yet He has made their salvation to depend upon impossible conditions. Indeed, many seem to think that the conduct and claims of God are always the components of a complicated fabric of contradiction, absurdity, and hypocrisy. But all such ideas of God are a libel on His infinitely fair and upright conduct.

There is nothing unkind or unnecessarily severe in the conduct of God toward the inhabitants of this world. There has been a great deal of complaint about His conduct among sinners; they have often complained of the injustice of His dealings and have sometimes inquired what they had done that He should chastise them with such severity. But all such complaining only proves their own perverseness and can never fasten any just suspicion upon the conduct of God.

Why Sinners Hate God

He Is Holy

Sinners do hate God because they are supremely selfish, and He is holy, which makes Him infinitely opposed to their supreme object of pursuit. Holiness is a regard for what is right. God requires, upon infinite penalties, every moral being in the universe to do, feel, and say what is perfectly right. He cannot require less than this without injustice. But sinners are unwilling to do right. They would rather be at liberty to consult their own private interests in everything, and they of course consider God as an enemy, because He insists upon their unqualified obedience to the law of right no matter how it counteracts their selfish schemes.

It is quite obvious that a proper desire to gratify an appetite for food, drink, and all our natural appetites is not sinful. These appetites have no moral character, and their proper indulgence is not sinful. But whenever their indulgence is inordinate, or whenever the indulgence of our appetites collides with the requirements of God; whenever we indulge our physical inclinations even though we are under an obligation to abstain from an indulgence, in every such case, we sin. In all these cases, we are selfish because we make our own indulgence, instead of the requirement of God, the rule by which we live. We agree to indulge ourselves in a way that is inconsistent with the glory of God and the highest good of His universe. This is the essence and the history of all sin.

Now, it is perhaps impossible for us to determine the exact point of our existence at which we first prefer self-gratification above our duty to God. But whenever this may be, this is the beginning of our depravity. It is our first moral act. It constitutes the beginnings of our moral character. Everything that has preceded this has had no moral character at all. The Bible assures us that this occurs so early in our lives that it may be said, *"The wicked are estranged from the womb; they go astray as soon as they are born, speaking lies"* (Psalm 58:3).

Of course, we do not speak at all as soon as we are born, but the wicked speak lies as soon as they do speak. The psalmist said, *"Behold, I was brought forth in iniquity, and in sin my mother conceived me"* (Psalm 51:5). This is figurative language, for it cannot be possible that the substance of a conceived fetus should be sin! This would contradict God's own definition of sin. He says, *"Sin is the transgression of the law"* (1 John 3:4 KJV). The law prescribes guidelines for action, not a mode of existence. If the substance of a conceived fetus is sin; if the child itself, prior to birth, is a sin, then God has committed it. All that can possibly be meant by this and similar passages—without making utter nonsense of the Word of God, without causing passages to contradict each other—is that we were always sinners from the beginning of our moral existence and from the earliest moment of the exercise of moral choice.

To insist upon a literal understanding of these and similar passages is the most dangerous perversion of the Bible. A literal interpretation proves not only that sin and holiness are substances, but also that God is a material being. Indeed, this has been the great error on the subject of depravity. All the language of the Bible is to be understood in its particular context. But this rule has been overlooked, and the same meaning has often been attached to the same word, no matter what the context might be. For instance, to set aside God's definition of sin, which is that sin is entirely a transgression of law, and to bring in figurative expressions that define sin as something other than voluntary transgression, is to make Scripture contradict itself by overlooking one of the most important rules of biblical interpretation.

Now, the great reason why sinners are opposed to God is not that there is any defect in their nature, making their opposition physically necessary, but because God is irreconcilably opposed to their selfishness. He is infinitely opposed to the supreme end of their pursuit, that is, to their obtaining happiness in a way that is inconsistent with His glory and the happiness of other beings. God is also opposed to the wicked means that they use to accomplish their end. These means make up the history of their lives. They are all designed, directly or indirectly, to bring about the all-absorbing objective at which the sinner aims: the promotion of his own happiness. God is therefore, as He ought to be, sincerely and infinitely opposed to everything they do or say while they remain impenitent.

God accordingly and purposely positions Himself to defeat every attempt that these people make to obtain happiness in their own way. He is the irreconcilable adversary of all their selfish schemes. He embitters every cup of selfish joy, turns their selfish counsel upon them (see Job 5:13), and brings down their violent dealings upon their own heads. (See Psalm 7:16.)

Thus you see that sinners hate God because He is so holy. While they remain selfish and He remains infinitely benevolent, their characters, their intentions, their desires, and all their ways are diametrically opposed to His, and His to theirs. They are direct opposites to Him; and until they change, it will always be true as He has said: "I loathe them, and they abhor me."

He Is Good

Second, sinners hate God because He is so good. He is good and does good, and He does everything to promote the public interest in a way that often overturns and scatters all their selfish projects and Babel-towers upon which they are attempting to climb to heaven. His heart is so set upon doing good that, in the pursuit of His great plan, He has often overthrown families and nations that stood in His way. Once, He overwhelmed a world of sinners in a flood to prevent their rebellion and to bring the world back to such a state that He might reclaim mankind and save a multitude from hell through the Gospel. (See Genesis 6–8.)

He Is Impartial

Sinners hate God because He is impartial. They view their own interests as supremely important and do all they can to make everything in the universe accommodate them. They would have the weather, the winds, and the whole material and moral universe conform to their purposes in order to complete and perpetuate their own happiness. But as God's purpose is entirely different from theirs, as His objective is to promote the general happiness and the happiness of individuals insofar as is consistent with the happiness and rights of other beings, He continually thwarts their efforts. The very elements of the material universe are so arranged and governed that their fondest hopes are often shipwrecked, and even their most fondly cherished expectations are annihilated.

He Threatens to Punish Sinners

But this is not all. Fourth, sinners hate God because He threatens to punish them for their sins. He will not compromise with them; He insists upon either their obedience or their damnation. He requires their repentance and reformation or the everlasting destruction of their souls. Now, either alternative is supremely hateful to an impenitent sinner. To repent, to confess that God is right and he is wrong; to take God's part against himself; to give up the pursuit of his own happiness as the supreme object of desire; to dedicate himself with all he is and has to the service of God and the promotion of the public interest is what he is utterly unwilling to do. But God insists upon it and will make no compromise. He demands unqualified and unconditional submission to His will or the eternal damnation of the person's soul. The sinner cannot reconcile himself to either. He considers God as his infinite and almighty Adversary, and he makes war upon Him with all his heart.

Sinners Hate What They Should Love

Sinners hate God for the very reasons for which they ought to love Him. These are the very reasons for which all holy beings do love Him. His opposition to all sin and to all harmful conduct; His high regard for individual and general happiness; and, in short, all the reasons for which selfish beings are so much opposed to Him are the foundations of obligation to love Him. These are the very reasons why reasonable beings, who have any regard for the moral fitness of things, feel it is right and feel it is their duty to love their Maker. He deserves to be loved for these reasons.

And it is for these and no other reasons that sinners hate Him. They do not hate Him because He deserves their hatred, but because He deserves their love. It is not because He is wicked, but because He is good. It is not because they have any good reason to hate Him, but because they have every possible reason to love

Him. I mean just what I say. Not only is it true that these reasons for loving Him do not prevent their hating Him, but they are the very reasons for which they hate Him.

Remarks

1. *From this subject, first of all, you can see the ridiculous hypocrisy of infidels.* It is very common for them to claim, in their investigations and inquiries after truth, to be impartial. They insist that Christians are already committed and are therefore incapable of giving Christianity a candid, unbiased, and reliable examination. Conversely, infidels seem to suppose that they are in circumstances that make up an unbiased and enlightened judgment and can examine and decide without prejudice. But this is utterly absurd. They are not on neutral ground, as they suppose themselves to be. Infidels are entirely opposed to God and are totally depraved. They are committed to being against the Bible. Their conduct, entirely irrespective of the Bible, proves that they are the enemies of God. It is clear that their lives can only be abhorred by God because He is holy. One needs no Bible to prove this.

Now, the Bible claims to be a revelation from God, demanding their holiness of heart and life and threatening them for their sins with eternal death. Is it not therefore absurd, ridiculous, and hypocritical for these enemies of God, committed as they are against God and against this Revelation, to declare themselves to be the only impartial judges?

They say they can investigate the subject without bias and that they are on neutral ground. They claim to feel no prejudice that would misguide their judgment. The fact is, Christians are not as prejudiced in favor of Christianity as infidels say they are. Until Christians are entirely perfect, they will not be so completely biased in favor of God as sinners are in favor of the Devil, nor will they be as likely to misjudge in favor of the Bible as sinners will be against it.

Overall, Christians favor God and therefore feel a strong attachment to the Bible. Yet much sin remains in them. Therefore, because they are likely to have many objections to the strictness of its claims, they are in the best circumstances and in the most favorable state of mind of any beings in the world to judge impartially. They are not so wicked that they reject what they see to be true, nor do they blindly submit to everything that pretends to have a claim upon their obedience. By this I do not mean that Christians are better qualified to judge the truth of the Christian religion now than when they will be perfect, but I do mean to repel the absurd assertions of infidels that the Christian's faith is nothing more than a blind credulity.

2. *From this subject, you can see that the wicked conduct of sinners is no proof that their human nature is sinful.* The universal sinfulness of men has been supposed to lead to the inevitable conclusion that the nature of man must be in itself sinful. It has been said that the universal sinful conduct of men can be accounted for in no other way. It has also been maintained that an effect must be of the same nature as its cause and that human nature must be sinful because the actions of that nature are universally sinful.

But if the effect must be of the same nature as its cause, and vice versa, then God must be a material being, for He is the cause of the existence of all matter. The mind of man must also be material, because it acts upon his material body and causes his body to act upon other material things around him. Because it is constantly bringing about material changes, the soul must also be material. This would, indeed, be a shorthand method of disposing of the existence of all spirits. But who will adopt as a serious and grave truth the absurd dogma that the character of an effect always decides the character or nature of its cause?

The universally sinful conduct of men is easily and naturally accounted for in the principles I related in the previous chapter. Human beings universally adopt the principle of selfishness as their grand rule of action from the very beginning. This impairs all their moral conduct and gives a sinful character to every moral action.

Someone may ask, "Why do children universally adopt the principle of selfishness, unless their nature is sinful?" They adopt this principle of self-gratification or selfishness because they possess human nature and are born under the circumstances in which all the children of Adam have been born since the Fall. But it is not because human nature is itself sinful. The cause of their becoming sinners is to be found in the fact that the world of sinners in which they live exposes them to the circumstances of temptation.

All the physical appetites and inclinations of the body and mind are in themselves innocent, but can become powerful temptations to indulge in what is prohibited. So many appeals of temptation are made to these physical appetites that it universally leads human beings to sin. Adam was created in the perfection of manhood, certainly not with a sinful nature, and yet an appeal to his innocent physical appetites led him into sin. Adult Adam, without a sinful nature and after a season of obedience and perfect holiness, was led to change his mind by an appeal to his innocent physical inclinations. Therefore, how can the fact that young children, possessing the same nature as Adam and surrounded by circumstances of still greater temptation, universally fall into sin, prove that their nature is itself sinful?

This is absurd philosophy, and what heightens its absurdity is that, in order to account for the sinfulness of human nature, we must believe that sin is found in the substance of the human body, instead of in voluntary action. And this would be impossible.

What gives this particular inference even more doubt is that, in making it, one rejects God's own declaration that "*sin is the transgression of the law*" (1 John 3:4 KJV) and adopts a definition that is perfectly absurd.

3. *From the view of depravity presented here, it is easy to see in what sense sin is natural to sinners and what has led mankind to ascribe the outbreakings of sin to its nature, as if its nature was itself sinful.* All experience shows that we are influenced in our conduct by the supreme preference of our minds. In other words, when we desire a thing supremely, it is natural for us to pursue this object of desire. We may have desires for an object that we do not pursue, but it is a contradiction to say that we do not pursue the object of our supreme desire. Just as the will controls the actions, so do we pursue the object that we supremely desire.

Therefore, the fact that sinners adopt the principle of supreme selfishness makes it certain and natural that they will sin while their selfishness continues to be predominant. This is in strict accordance with, or rather the result of, the laws of their minds. While they maintain their supreme selfishness, obedience is impossible. This is the reason why *"the carnal mind* [or the minding of the flesh]*...is not subject to the law of God, nor indeed can be"* (Romans 8:7). No wonder sinners, whose supreme preference is selfish, find it very natural to sin and extremely difficult to do anything else but sin.

This being a fact of universal observation, it has led people to ascribe the sins of mankind to human nature. And a great deal of fault has been found with human nature itself, when the fact is that sin is only an abuse of the powers of that nature. Men have very extensively overlooked the fact that a deep-seated but voluntary preference for sin was the foundation and cause of all other sins. The only sense in which sin is natural to men is that it is natural for the mind to be influenced by a supreme preference or choice for some object. Therefore, it will always be natural for a sinner to sin, until he changes the supreme preference of his mind and prefers the glory of God and the interests of His kingdom above his own separate and opposing interests.

4. *Here you can see what a change of heart is: its nature, its necessity, and the obligation of the sinner to change it immediately.* You can also see that the first act that the sinner can or will perform, that can be acceptable to God, is to change his heart and the supreme controlling preference of his mind.

5. *The hatred of sinners is cruel.* It is as God says: "*They have rewarded me…hatred for my love*" (Psalm 109:5). He is love, and this is the reason and the only reason why they hate Him. Indeed, it is not because they overlook the fact that He is infinitely benevolent. They do not hate Him for other reasons in the face of this fact, but it is because of this fact. It is literally and absolutely rendering hatred for His love.

God is opposed to sinners' injuring each other. He desires their happiness and is infinitely opposed to their making themselves miserable. He is infinitely more opposed to their doing anything that will prove injurious to themselves—even more than an earthly parent is opposed to a course of conduct in his beloved child that he foresees will ruin him. God's heart yearns with infinitely more than parental tenderness. He expostulates with sinners and says, "*Oh, do not do this abominable thing that I hate!*" (Jeremiah 44:4).

> *How can I give you up, Ephraim? How can I hand you over, Israel? How can I make you like Admah? How can I set you like Zeboiim? My heart churns within Me; My sympathy is stirred.* (Hosea 11:8)

The Lord feels all the outpourings of a father's tenderness and all the opposition of a father to any course that will injure his offspring. Just as children will sometimes hate their parents for opposing their wayward courses to destruction, so sinners hate

God more than they hate all other beings, because He is infinitely more opposed to their destroying their souls.

6. *The better God is in sinners' estimations, the more they hate Him.* The better they see Him to be, the more they see that He is opposed to their selfishness; and the more they know Him to oppose their selfishness, while they remain selfish, the more they are provoked by Him.

In my second chapter on depravity, I showed that men hate God supremely. The only reason is that His excellence is supreme excellence. His goodness is unmingled goodness, and therefore their hatred is unmingled enmity. If there were any defect in His character, men would not hate Him so much. If God were not perfectly and infinitely good, men might not be totally depraved; I mean, they might not be totally opposed to His character. But because His character has no blemish, they sincerely, wholeheartedly, and perfectly hate Him.

7. *The more God tries to do good to sinners, while they remain impenitent, the more they will hate Him.* While they retain their selfishness, all His efforts are to restrain it, to hedge them in, to prevent the accomplishment of their selfish desires. The more He intervenes to tear away their idols, to wean them from the world, and the more means He uses to reclaim, sanctify, and save them, the more He embitters every cup of joy with which they attempt to satisfy themselves. If their selfishness remains unbroken, the more deeply and eternally will they hate Him.

8. *This conduct in sinners is infinitely blameworthy and deserves eternal death.* It is impossible to imagine guilt that is deeper and more damning than that of sinners under the Gospel. They sin under such peculiar circumstances that their guilt is more aggravated than that of devils. Devils have broken the law, and so have you, sinners. But devils never were given the opportunity of accepting or rejecting the Gospel. They have been guilty of rebellion, and

so have you. But they have never rejected the offer of pardon and spurned the offer of eternal life through the atoning blood of the Son of God. If you sinners do not deserve eternal death, I cannot imagine that there is a devil in hell that deserves it. And yet, strange to say, sinners often speak as if it were doubtful whether they deserve to be damned.

9. *It is easy to see from this subject that saints and angels will be entirely satisfied with the justice of God in the damnation of sinners.* They will never take delight in the misery of the damned, but only in the display of justice, in the vindication of His insulted majesty and injured honor. They will have pleasure in the respect that punishment will create for the law and character of God. They will see that the display of His justice is glorious and will cry "Hallelujah" while *"the smoke of their torment ascends forever and ever"* (Revelation 14:11).

Seven

God Cannot Please Sinners

And the Lord said, "To what then shall I liken the men of this generation, and what are they like? They are like children sitting in the marketplace and calling to one another, saying: 'We played the flute for you, and you did not dance; we mourned to you, and you did not weep.' For John the Baptist came neither eating bread nor drinking wine, and you say, 'He has a demon.' The Son of Man has come eating and drinking, and you say, 'Look, a glutton and a winebibber, a friend of tax collectors and sinners!' But wisdom is justified by all her children."
—Luke 7:31–35

It would seem as if God intended, in His dealings with men, to leave them without excuse. He uses such a variety of ways to reclaim and save them, that it appears as if He meant to try every possible means of winning them away from death, so that He might give them eternal life.

John the Baptist was a simple and somber man. He seemed to have very little dealings with the people except in his public capacity as a prophet. His message was one of reproof and rebuke in a high degree. His diet was locusts and wild honey, and he seemed to practice a high degree of austerity in all his habits of living. He was not a public teacher in Jerusalem, but he proclaimed his message in the wildest parts of Judea, to which the people flocked to listen to his instruction. His habits of life, his style of preaching, his abstaining in a great measure from dealings with the people, led his enemies to say that he was possessed by a demon.

After the scribes and Pharisees had declined receiving John's doctrine, under the pretense that he had a demon, Jesus Christ began His public ministry. In His habits of life and dealings with the people, He differed widely from John the Baptist. Instead of confining Himself to the wilderness of Judea, he visited most of the principal places. He also spent considerable time in Jerusalem as a public teacher. He was generally pleasant; He mingled with great ease and holy civility with almost all classes of individuals, for the purpose of instructing them in the great doctrines of salvation. He did not hesitate to accept the invitations of the Pharisees and great men of the nation to dine with them, and on all occasions He directly administered whatever reproof and instruction were required by the circumstances and characters of those with whom He associated.

But when the Pharisees listened to His doctrines, they were filled with indignation. They saw His easy and gentlemanly manner, but they called Him a gluttonous man, a drunkard, and a friend of tax collectors and sinners. They opposed John, claiming that he was morose and sour, that he had a denunciatory spirit and was therefore possessed by a demon. And they opposed Christ on opposite grounds: that He was too friendly and familiar with all classes of people, especially tax collectors and sinners. It was this inconsistency in them that drew forth from Christ the words of the verse quoted above.

The text verse alludes to Eastern customs: to their seasons of festivity and dancing on the one hand, and to their loud lamentation and mournings at funerals on the other. As everyone knows, it is common for little children at play to copy things that adults do. When they see festivals and dancing and hear the music being

God Cannot Please Sinners   149

played, they find something that will suffice as a musical instrument and go around playing the instrument and dancing, imitating what they have seen. Similarly, when they have witnessed funerals at which the loud wails of mourning men and women have excited great lamentations among the spectators, as is common in the East, they have attempted to copy this, too.

Christ compared the conduct of the scribes and Pharisees to children who sit in the marketplaces and complain that their little playfellows are morose and sour and unwilling to play with them. When they imitated festivity and dancing, their playfellows were solemn and reserved and did not seem disposed to merriment. And when they attempted to play something that was more mournful by wailing to them as if at a funeral, then they were inclined to be merry. *"We played the flute for you,"* they said, *"and you did not dance; we mourned to you, and you did not weep"* (Luke 7:32). When Christ had told His audience about the conduct of these children, He then explained their own actions to them:

> For John the Baptist came neither eating bread nor drinking wine, and you say, "He has a demon." The Son of Man has come eating and drinking, and you say, "Look, a glutton and a winebibber, a friend of tax collectors and sinners!" But wisdom is justified by all her children.   (Luke 7:33–35)

With these words, I will illustrate the proposition that God cannot please sinners.

Conflict Between the Heart and the Conscience

Some people imagine that a misrepresentation of God's character has created much of the opposition to Him in this world. Sometimes His character is greatly misrepresented, and when His character is misrepresented, the consciences of men are opposed to

Him. But even when His character is truly represented, they are still not pleased, and their hearts remain opposed to Him.

The fact is, sinners are at continual war with themselves. Their hearts and consciences are in perpetual opposition to each other. One view of a subject will please their hearts but offend their consciences, and another view of it will satisfy their consciences but arouse the enmity of their hearts. While they are in this state, it is clearly impossible to please them. To illustrate this proposition, I will make a few observations.

Regarding God's Holiness

First, sinners do not like the holiness of God, nor would they like Him if He were unholy. To the holiness of God their hearts are bitterly opposed. To deny this is as absurd as it is false. To say that an impenitent heart is not opposed to holiness is the same as to say that an impenitent heart is not impenitent. Impenitence is the love of sin, and sin and holiness are direct opposites. God is infinitely holy, and therefore the impenitent heart is entirely opposed to Him.

But suppose God were infinitely sinful. Would sinners be better pleased with Him than they are at present? No. They would then make war upon Him because He was so wicked. Their consciences would then condemn Him, and although their hearts would be appeased, their consciences and their better judgment would be utterly opposed to Him. Human nature is such that men cannot approve the character of a wicked being. No man has ever fully approved of the character of the Devil, and wicked men are opposed to both God and the Devil for opposite reasons. They hate God with their hearts because He is so holy; and in their consciences they condemn the Devil because he is so wicked.

Suppose you place the character of God at any point between the two extremes of infinite holiness and infinite sinfulness. Sinners still would not be better pleased with Him than they are now. Inasmuch as He was holy, their hearts would hate Him. Inasmuch as He was wicked, their consciences would condemn Him. In this way, He does not please them as He is, nor would He please them if He were to change.

Regarding God's Justice

Second, sinners do not like the justice of God, nor would they like Him if He were unjust. There is hardly anything in the character of God that is more revolting to an impenitent heart than the awful justice that threatens sinners with eternal death. But if God were unjust, then their consciences would condemn Him. Now, place Him anywhere between the extremes of infinite justice and infinite injustice. To the degree that He was just, their hearts would hate Him; and to the degree that He was unjust, their consciences would condemn Him.

Regarding God's Mercy

Third, sinners do not like the mercy of God when they see the conditions upon which it is to be exercised. However, they would not like God if He were unmerciful. If they liked His mercy with its conditions, they would accept forgiveness and would no longer be impenitent sinners. But if God were unmerciful, then they would certainly be opposed to Him.

Regarding God's Law

Fourth, they do not like the requirement of His law as it now stands, nor would they approve of it if it were altered. When they behold its perfection, their hearts rise up against it. But if it were imperfect and allowed some degree of sin, their consciences would condemn it. Let the requirement of the law remain as it is, or alter it as you will, and sinners are and will be displeased. The law now requires perfect holiness, and for this reason the sinner's heart is entirely opposed to it. But suppose the law required entire sinfulness.

Then the sinner's conscience would utterly condemn it. And what if it were of a mixed character, requiring some holiness and some sin? Inasmuch as it required holiness, their hearts would hate it; and inasmuch as it required sin, their consciences would condemn it. Overall, they would be as far from being satisfied as they are now.

Regarding the Penalty for Sin

Fifth, sinners do not like the penalty of the law as it now stands, nor would they approve of it if it were altered. The hearts of sinners rise into most outrageous rebellion when the penalty of eternal death is held out before them. But if the penalty were less, their consciences would condemn it. Then they would say the penalty was not equal to the importance of the precept. Because the requirement is infinite, they would say it is a plain matter of common sense that the penalty should be infinite. They would insist that God is under an obligation to deal out the penalty that carries the same weight as the requirement. Furthermore, they would say that God has not done everything possible to prevent the commission of sin, that He has not presented the highest reasons for obedience that could be presented, and that He is therefore deficient in benevolence and even lacking in common honesty and justice.

Now, place the penalty of this law at any point between eternal death and no penalty at all, and the sinner is still not satisfied. If you make it less than eternal death, you offend his conscience; and if you let it remain as it is, you offend his heart.

Regarding the Gospel

Sixth, sinners do not like the Gospel as it now stands, nor would they be better satisfied if it were altered. They do not like the rule of conduct that the Gospel prescribes, nor would they be satisfied if it prescribed any other rule. It requires that men be holy, as God is holy, and it requires the same strictness and perfection as the moral law does. This is a great offense to their hearts. But

if it prescribed a different rule of conduct and lowered its requirements in order to suit the sinful inclinations of men, then their
consciences would oppose it. "What sort of Gospel is this?" they
would ask. To this their consciences would entirely object.

Sinners also do not like the conditions of the Gospel, nor
would they be satisfied if those conditions were altered. The conditions are repentance and faith, but to these the sinner's heart is
opposed. To hate his sins, to trust in Christ for salvation, is asking
too much to obtain the consent of his heart. But suppose the
Gospel offered to pardon and save without requiring repentance
and faith. To this the sinner's conscience and common sense would
object. "What?" he would say. "Can the Gospel offer pardon while
men continue their rebellion? Will men be saved in their sins? It
is absurd and impossible. And will men be saved without faith in
Christ? Will they be received and pardoned while they make God
a liar? Will they go to heaven without believing there is a heaven?
Will they escape hell when they do not believe there is a hell? Will
they ever find their way to everlasting life when they have no confidence in the testimony of God and will not walk in the only way
that will conduct them there? Impossible! A Gospel that pretends
to save on such conditions must be from hell."

Now suppose the conditions of the Gospel remain as they are,
or suppose they are altered in any way. Either way, the sinner is not
satisfied. When left as they are, the conditions of the Gospel agree
with his conscience but are a great offense to his heart. If they are
altered, so as to appease his heart, his conscience is offended. Thus,
while the sinner remains impenitent, there is no conceivable alteration that will please him.

Regarding Ministers of the Gospel

Seventh, sinners do not like the doctrines that ministers
preach when they preach the truth, nor would they be satisfied

if error was preached to them. If preachers speak forth the pure doctrines of the Gospel and bear down upon the hearts and consciences of men with the claims of God, sinners' hearts arise in instant rebellion. "This," they say, "is an abominable doctrine." But if the ministers dismiss the high claims of the Gospel, sinners' consciences are dissatisfied, and those who are well instructed say that the ministers are afraid to tell the truth, that they are deceiving the people and leading them down to hell.

Now, whether the minister preaches the whole truth or error or a mixture of the two, the sinner's heart opposes it and his conscience condemns it. So let the minister preach what he will; while the sinner is impenitent, he will never be completely satisfied.

Sinners do not like the way many ministers preach, nor would they be satisfied if their manner were different. If the minister's manner is rousing and impressive, the sinner's heart rises up against it. If it is lazy and cold and dry, his conscience condemns it. In the first case, the sinner says, "That minister is a fanatic and a madman for appealing to the passions and for exciting people's fleshly emotions. He frightens people and will drive people to madness." In the latter case, he says that the minister puts the people to sleep, that he is dull and does not believe the Gospel himself. Now, whether the minister's manner is right or wrong or a mixture of the two, the sinner is not satisfied. Insofar as the manner is right, his conscience takes sides against it; and while the sinner is so inconsistent with himself, it is in vain to hope to please him.

Sinners do not like the lives of ministers, nor would they be satisfied if the ministers lived differently. If a minister is determined to know nothing *"except Jesus Christ and Him crucified"* (1 Corinthians 2:2), if he makes religion his entire business and talks about his message all the time, the sinner's heart is filled with indignation. The sinner says, "This man is a bigot, full of superstition." Or he calls him a hypocrite and says, "He is not as sociable and affable as a minister ought to be. He takes no interest in the common concerns of men, is entirely unacquainted with human nature, and is always intruding his religion upon everyone. Wouldn't a minister do more good if he were more like other people?"

But, on the other hand, if the minister associates with the world like other people, takes an interest in the passing occurrences of the day, tells stories and is cheerful, companionable, and at home among his people, then the sinner's conscience condemns him. He says, "I don't see that he is any better than anybody else. He is not what a minister should be, but is fond of politics and is as much interested in the business of this world as other people are. I like to see a minister confine himself to the duties of his office." Now, whether the minister lives rightly or wrongly, the sinner is displeased.

But suppose there is a mixture of consistency and inconsistency, or right and wrong, in a minister's life. Then the sinner will say, "He is not at all what he should be. Sometimes he is very hot, sometimes very cold. Sometimes he is all religion, and sometimes no religion. This will only bring hurt and harm, for a minister should be consistent and always the same." Now, it is evident that, while the sinner is so inconsistent with himself, he will be displeased with the lives of ministers, no matter how they may live. Inasmuch as the minister lives as he should, the impenitent heart loathes him, and inasmuch as he lives as he should not, the sinner's conscience condemns him.

Regarding the Conduct of Christians

Eighth, sinners do not like the conduct of Christians, nor would they be satisfied if it were different. When Christians are very much engaged in religion, have many meetings, and make great efforts to save the souls of men, the hearts of sinners are very much disturbed. They call them fanatics and hypocrites and think they had better attend to their worldly business. Sinners think Christians are intrusive for going from house to house and forcing their religion upon all their neighbors. They say that Christians who are opposed to parties and other kinds of amusements are morose and misanthropic; that they are opposed to all the sympathies and courtesies of life; and that they want to make everybody else as morose and unhappy as they are.

Sinners say, "Wouldn't Christians do better to engage in something else than in muttering their prayers, running to meetings, and exhorting their neighbors to repent, as if nobody had any religion but themselves?" But suppose, on the other hand, that Christians say very little about religion, seldom attend meetings except on Sundays, engage as deeply in business as worldly men, and appear to enjoy parties and time-killing amusements. Sinners would say, "These people who claim to be Christians are all hypocrites. What do they do more than others? They care nothing about the souls of their neighbors. They neither warn them nor exhort them, nor do they live as if they believed there was a heaven or a hell. If these are Christians, I want no such religion as this."

Thus, whether Christians live rightly or wrongly, sinners are not satisfied. Or, if there is a mixture of good and evil in their lives, sinners are no better pleased. If Christians sometimes do their duty, and at other times neglect it, sinners say that their inconsistency is a great stumbling block, that they don't like this periodical religion, that it is one day all zeal and the next all coldness and death. The truth is, if Christians are zealous, the sinner's heart is disturbed; and if they are cold, his conscience passes judgment against them. Who can please these sinners?

Regarding Church Practices

Ninth, sinners are displeased if the church exercises discipline and dismisses unworthy members, and they are also displeased if the church does not do it. If a church allows disorderly and wicked people to take Communion, sinners' consciences are opposed to this. They say these church members are all hypocrites, to sanction such conduct as this. The church can never prosper while it retains fellowship with such hypocrites. By having fellowship with wicked people, the church shows that its members approve the wicked deeds. But on the other hand, if the church rises up and excommunicates these offending members, then the hearts of sinners are disturbed. They maintain that the church is persecuting some of its best members. They think that the proceedings of the church are very uncharitable to deal thusly with people who, for all they can see, are as good as anyone else in the church.

Cases of this kind have occurred in which the excommunicated members have been advised, by the ungodly, to sue the church for slander. The truth is, while sinners continue to be so inconsistent with themselves, nothing about religion can please them. What is right offends their hearts, and what is wrong offends their consciences.

Thus you see that it is of no use for God to try to please you, sinner, while you are in your sins. He could not please you if He wanted to, and He would not please you if He could while you remain in sin. Sinners often seem to imagine that if God were the kind of being that they desire Him to be, they would love Him. They do not realize, however, that if they framed a God to suit their hearts, they would fail to appease their consciences. Sinner, your conscience approves of the character of God as it is. If His character could be altered to any conceivable degree, it would not please you any better than it does now while you are in your sins. For if you could alter His character so that it satisfies your heart, you would only outrage your conscience; and the only possible way for you to be happy is to change yourself instead of expecting or desiring God to change.

Remarks

1. *It is impressive to see how many people make continual efforts to hide themselves behind some "refuge of lies" (Isaiah 28:17).* They want to believe what is agreeable to their feelings, even if they are wrong. In the wild uproar of their tumultuous feelings, the voice of conscience is drowned, and for the time being sinners relax in their sins. But when the tumult of feeling subsides and an enlightened conscience can be heard, it gives forth the sentence of condemnation against their favorite heresy. Conscience comes forth and writes *falsehood* upon it in plain view. This leads the heart to mutiny, and an internal war is created, from which it would seem that the sinner can only escape by working himself into such an excitement that he loses sight of Scripture and reason and common sense.

People of almost every description seem to act this way; they seem to be unhappy unless they can be engaged in some exciting conversation that will drown the voice of conscience. But until they have violently silenced their consciences, they can never rest quietly in any form of error when they have been rightly instructed. It is futile for them to expect to bring an enlightened conscience to take sides against truth and against God. God has not left Himself without a witness in the sinner's heart, and however much his warring passions and his desperate heart may mutiny against high heaven, the sinner may rest assured that conscience will write and sign and seal his death warrant. And, in anticipation of coming retribution, conscience will hand the sinner over to the executioner of eternal justice.

This is why sinners will at one time praise, and at another condemn, the same thing. Suppose a sinner goes to hear a minister preach who makes falsehood appear like truth and truth like falsehood. He conceals the sinner's danger; he says nothing of his guilt. He *"strengthen[s] the hands of the wicked, so that he does not turn from his wicked way to save his life"* (Ezekiel 13:22). "Oh," says the sinner, "what a charming preacher!" And he goes home pouring forth the most enthusiastic compliments for the sermon. But when his feelings subside, when he has had time for reflection, and when he has thought about it, he will change his tune. Then his conscience will condemn the preacher and his sermon as something meant to bewitch and deceive, rather than to reform and save.

But when he hears a minister who speaks the truth of God with the most impressive pungency, the sinner's heart will rise in rebellion. He will pour out curses upon the minister and his sermon and declare that he will never hear him preach again. He is ready to quarrel with everyone who tries to justify the sermon or the preacher. But let him have time to cool, let his conscience have its work, and you will find him speaking a different language. He will say, after all, "I may as well go and hear this preacher again; the man preached the truth, and I may as well hear it as not. Though I was angry at his doctrine, I cannot but respect his honesty; I will go once more and hear what he has to say."

Now, in one of these cases the sinner speaks the language of his heart, and in the other the language of his conscience. Thus you can see that a minister whose preaching pleases the hearts of sinners cannot commend himself to their consciences in the sight of God. (See 2 Corinthians 5:11.) Many ministers seem to aim at appeasing the impenitent members of their congregations. They seem to consider it a proof of their wisdom and prudence when their preaching has much favor with the ungodly. But as soon as these sinners are converted, they lose their confidence in such a minister. Their consciences, if enlightened, tell them that they have never been satisfied with him. They have praised his preaching and loved to hear him because he has pleased their hearts but not their consciences.

If they are ever truly converted and their hearts agree with their consciences, it is highly probable that they will go away and join some other congregation, if another is within their reach. And in cases where they do not do this, there is reason to fear that they are not truly converted. But where a minister preaches to the conscience and where sinners get angry and go away, if they are ever converted they will desire to come back again and listen to the preaching that used to disturb them while they were in their sins.

2. *From this subject, you can see that where Christians try to influence sinners by using religion to appease the sinners' feelings while they are in their sins, they will never do the sinners any good.* For though this may please the hearts of sinners, their consciences condemn them; and while their consciences condemn the course they take, it is impossible that this course can do them any good.

Many Christians attempt to gain influence with sinners by imitating them and conforming to their lives, habits, and tastes. In this way, they seem to think that they will gain access to them and influence over them. But it is certain that the access and influence they will thus gain will never do the sinner any good, because the whole course of conduct by which this influence is gained is condemned by the sinner's conscience. It is not a religious influence, but a worldly one, that is thus gained. It is not a sanctified influence, but a sinful one. And instead of giving weight to the character of the person who takes this course as a Christian, it has the directly opposite effect. It destroys the confidence of the sinner that the person is a Christian. By taking this proud and worldly course to gain influence, the Christian may appease the sinner's feelings and please his heart, but the sinner's conscience repels and condemns him.

3. *God speaks and conducts Himself in such a way as to commend Himself to every man's conscience.* The sinner's heart is entirely opposed to God, but God pursues a course that does not leave Himself without a witness. Conscience will testify for God. Now, the sinner's heart must certainly be reconciled to God, or he is eternally

miserable; his judgment and conscience will always bear witness that God is right. Unless the heart is brought over to take sides with the conscience, it is obvious that the sinner must be damned.

Ministers and other Christians should take the same course that God does, and should live and speak in a way that will satisfy the sinner's conscience. If we live so as to have the sinner's conscience on our side, however much he may hate us now, he will certainly love us or be damned. If we have done what his conscience approves of, he will be reconciled to us, or else God will never be reconciled to him.

4. *You see why people who are converted often show the greatest attachment to those Christians whom they most hated prior to their conversion.* Christians who lead the holiest lives are most apt to be hated by impenitent sinners; and it often happens that the more these Christians reprove and warn and rebuke them, the more the sinners will hate them. But if the sinners become truly converted, they will almost certainly have the highest confidence in those very individuals. This is because their hearts are changed. Their consciences took sides with the faithful Christians before, and now that they are converted, both hearts and consciences approve the Christians' character.

5. *You see from this subject why, when people are converted, they show the least attachment for and the least confidence in those apparently religious people with whom they were most intimate while in their sins.* Those with whom they were most pleased, while in this state of impenitence, were agreeable to them not because they had so much piety but because they had so little, not because they did their duty to them so faithfully but because they neglected it. Now, when these sinners are converted, they cannot have much confidence in the piety of those religious people with whom they used to have this kind of worldly intimacy. They cannot help suspecting that they have no piety.

6. You see that negotiating with sinners—softening, concealing, or evading the claims of the Gospel—can do them no good. To attempt to please them while they are in their sins can only ruin them. Their hearts must be changed, and the only way to bring this about is to take the deepest hold of the conscience that is possible. Instead of expecting to change the heart by concealing the offensive features of the Gospel, we need to change it by presenting the conscience with the claims of God, in all their dimensions. The heart will be brought over, with the aid of the conscience, and the more fully the claims of God are presented to the conscience, the more likely the sinner is to be converted.

To conceal the truth from a person's conscience, or to attempt to win the sinner over by a lovely song, is only going to lull him with the voice of a temptress until he plunges into eternal death.

7. You see from this subject why convicted sinners often show the greatest opposition just before they submit to God. It is often the case that the more the conscience is pressed, the more the sinner frets and rebels. When the conscience is thoroughly enlightened and has obtained a firm enough footing to exert its utmost power upon the heart, a desperate conflict often ensues. Then, in the madness of his exasperated feelings, the sinner is sometimes almost ready to blaspheme the God of heaven. And it is often here, while their consciences are taking their most thorough lessons from the truth and Spirit of God, that the enmity of sinners breaks out with its greatest power. The power of truth, presented by the Spirit of God, exerts upon the heart such tremendous power through the conscience that the sinner is made to throw down his weapons and submit to God.

8. From this subject, you can see the longsuffering of God in sparing sinners. How amazing it is that He spares them so long, despite all their unreasonable faultfinding and rebellion! Nothing that He does pleases them, and nothing that He can do would please them.

What would you think of your children if they were to act this way toward you? Suppose they had never obeyed you and had never so much as meant to obey you: when you acted in such a way as to please their consciences, their hearts opposed you; and when you pleased their hearts, their consciences opposed you. Overall, you have not pleased them and cannot. They are always displeased and murmuring at whatever you do. Even the kindest earthly parents would have little patience with their children when compared with the longsuffering of the blessed God.

9. *It is futile for sinners to wait for God to use means that suit them better before they are converted.* Most sinners are waiting to hear some different kind of preaching, and sometimes they will go from one revival to another because the means, they think, are not adapted to their case. Sometimes they hear preaching that pleases their hearts, but then their consciences are not enough impressed to do them any good. Or they hear preaching that impresses their consciences, but their hearts rise up in rebellion.

Now, they think that if they could only hear some preaching, or if God could use some means, that would please both their consciences and their hearts, they would be converted. But such means cannot possibly be used while the heart and conscience are opposed to each other. Sinner, there is no use in your waiting. To expect God or anybody else to satisfy you before you are converted is vain; and if you wait for such an event, you will wait until you are in the depths of hell.

Sinners should not desire that means be used to please their hearts while they are in their sins. If any preaching or means makes you feel pleasant, if your heart is delighted by it, rest assured that these means will do you no good. They will only deceive you and make you overlook the necessity of a change of heart.

10. *You can see the nature of hell's torments.* Sinners are often thrown into great agony in this life by the internal struggles of their

164 Sermons on Important Subjects

consciences and hearts. Suppose they go into eternity with their hearts unchanged, and the full blaze of eternity's light is poured upon their consciences. With a heart at enmity against God, what horrible rebellion, what insupportable conflict and quarreling with self and with God, the sinner will experience! If his conscience sternly takes sides with God and his heart supremely hates Him, what a fire of hell such a conflict will kindle in the sinner!

11. *Lastly, sinners should not follow their feelings but should obey the voice of conscience.* In cases outside of religious matters, where sinners find their feelings opposed to their better judgment, they will often resist the current of their feelings. They will say, "I am not going to be carried away by my feelings. I must exercise my judgment. I must act like a reasonable being." But when it comes to spiritual matters, how perfectly men give themselves up to their wicked hearts! Sinner, you ought this moment to come forth and say you will not go another step in the way of death. Why throw up the reigns and give way to passion? Why drive with such furious haste to hell? Why allow yourself to be carried here and there by every rush of feeling and by every breath of emotion that passes over the surface of your soul?

Sinner, if you do not exercise your reason, if you do not listen to the voice of conscience, if you do not gather up the reigns and address yourself to the work of your salvation, if you do not make up your mind to resist the whole tide of your carnal feelings and put yourself under the clear blaze of heaven's light, when conscience gives forth its verdict, you will die in your sins unless you will promptly obey. Will you do this while danger is before you, while mercy waits to save and death brandishes his weapon to destroy, while heaven calls and hell groans, while the Spirit strives and Christians pray? Will you have the moral courage, the decision of character, and the honesty to resolve on immediate submission to Jesus Christ?

Eight

Christian Affinity

Can two walk together, unless they are agreed?
—Amos 3:3

In the Holy Scriptures, we often find a negative statement put in the form of a question. The above verse is an instance of this. We are to understand the prophet as affirming that two cannot walk together unless they agree on where they are going.

When two people truly agree, they must agree in more than just theory or understanding. We often see people who agree in theory but who differ vastly in feeling and practice. Their minds may embrace the same truth, while their hearts and practices will be very differently affected by it. Saints and sinners often embrace the same religious creed in theory, while it is plain that they differ widely in feeling and practice. We have reason to believe that angels and devils understand and embrace the same truths intellectually, and yet they are affected by them very differently.

These different effects, produced in different minds by the same truths, are owing to the different states of the hearts or emotions of the different individuals. In other words, the difference in the effect is found in the different manner in which each person receives these truths or feels and acts in light of them. I have observed that the same truths will affect the same person very differently at different times. This, too, is owing to the different state of the emotions at these times and to the different manner in which the mind acts at these times.

All pleasure and pain, all happiness and misery, all sin and holiness, are centered in and belong to the heart or feelings. All the satisfaction or dissatisfaction, pain or pleasure, depends entirely upon the state of our emotions at the time. If something contributes to pleasurable emotions, we are of course pleased, for our happiness consists in these pleasurable emotions. Therefore, the higher these emotions are elevated by the presentation of any truth to our minds, the greater our pleasure is.

But if the truth does not correspond to our current feelings, it cannot please us. If it is different from our present state of feeling and we refuse to change the course of our feelings, we will either view it with indifference or we will turn from and resist it. We feel uninterested or displeased and disgusted when a subject that differs from what presently engages our feelings is introduced and crowded upon us.

These are truths to which every man will testify. If you eloquently present the ardent politician with his favorite subject in his favorite light, when his feelings have been engaged, he will be greatly delighted. But change your style and tone, and present the subject in a drier light, and he immediately loses nearly all interest and becomes uneasy. Change the subject to that of death and solemn judgment, and he is shocked and stunned. Press him with such topics, and he is disgusted and offended.

Now, the disgust that he feels at the change of subject is the natural consequence of presenting something that is directly opposed to the state of his feelings. Unless he chooses to change his mind as you change the subject, he cannot help but be displeased.

A talented musician is listening almost in rapture to the skillful execution of a fine piece of harmony. The sounds of the musical instruments touch him in a tender spot in his heart, the music accords with his feelings, and so he is gratified. But throw in discord upon him, and he is in pain in a moment. Increase and prolong the dissonance, and he leaves the room in disgust.

Or suppose he is fond of music, but at the moment he is melancholy. He is in great affliction and is inclined to weep. His tears flow fast, he feels distressed, and so he turns away and plugs his ears when he hears joyful music. The music opposes his state of feeling; he is too melancholy to have his feelings elevated and enlivened by it; it therefore distresses him.

Suppose your heart is glowing with religious feelings. You are not only averse to the introduction of any other subject at this time, but you are also uninterested in anything upon the same subject that is far below the level of your feelings. Suppose, like Paul, you *"have great sorrow and continual grief in* [your] *heart"* (Romans 9:2) for dying sinners. In this state of mind, you hear a person pray who does not mention sinners, or you hear a minister preach who says very little to them, and that in a heartless, unmeaning manner. You are not interested in what he has to say; you cannot be, feeling as you do. Rather, you are grieved and distressed.

Suppose your feelings are lukewarm and carnal and earthly. You hear one exhort, pray, or preach, who is highly spiritual and fervent. If you cling to your sins and your feelings do not rise; if through prejudice or pride or the earthly and sensual state of your feelings you refuse to kindle and to grasp the subject, although you admit to the truth of every word he says, you will not be pleased. He is above your emotional temperature; you are annoyed with the manner, fire, and spirit of the man. The higher he rises, if your feelings remain where they are, the farther apart you are and the more you are displeased. While your heart is wrong, the nearer to right he is, the more his words will burn in your soul.

Now, those whose feelings stand at or near the same point as he who speaks or prays, will not feel disturbed but will be pleased. Those who are lukewarm will listen to the dull man and say that the man speaks well of good things. Their pleasure will be small, because their feelings are low, but overall they are pleased. Those who have no feelings at the time will, of course, not feel at all. All who have much feeling will listen with grief and pain. These wish to listen to the ardent man with great interest. Let him glow and blaze, and they are in a rapture. But the carnal and coldhearted, while they refuse to let their feelings rise, are necessarily disturbed and offended by his fire.

Remarks

1. *It is evident from this subject why people who differ in theory on doctrinal points in religion and who belong to different denominations will often, for a time, walk together in great harmony.* It is because they feel deeply and similarly. Their differences are mostly lost or forgotten while they fall in with each other's state of feeling; they will walk together while their hearts agree.

2. *You see why young converts love to associate with each other and with older saints who have a great deal of religious feeling.* These walk together because they feel alike.

3. *You see why impenitent sinners and those whose faith is lukewarm have the same difficulties with the means used in revivals.* We often hear them complain of the manner of preaching and praying. Their objections are the same; they find fault with the same things and use the same arguments in support of their objections. The reason is that, at that time, their feelings are nearly the same. It is the fire and the spirit that disturb their frosty hearts. For the time, they walk together, for in feeling they are agreed.

4. *This subject shows why ministers and other Christians who attend revivals often raise objections at first to the means used and sometimes take sides with the wicked.* The fact is, the praying, preaching, and conversation are most likely above their present spiritual

and emotional temperature. Sometimes there is prejudice if the revival is taking place within a different denomination from their own. Or perhaps prejudice against the preacher, or pride, envy, worldliness, or something of the kind, chains down their feelings so that they do not enter into the spirit of the work.

Now, while their hearts remain wrong, they will, of course, raise objections. And the more right a thing is, the more spiritual and holy, so much the more it must displease them while their feelings remain low.

5. *From this subject, it is evident why Christians differ about what is prudent in evangelism.* The man who sees and feels the infinitely solemn things of eternity will have a very different idea of what is prudent or imprudent in the use of means than one whose spiritual eye is almost closed. The man whose heart is breaking for perishing sinners will, of course, deem it prudent and right and necessary to use plain speech and to deal with sinners in a very earnest and affectionate manner. He would deem a contrary course highly imprudent, even dangerous. Meanwhile, he who has few feelings for sinners and sees only a little of their danger will satisfy himself with using very different means, or using them in a very different manner. He will, of course, entertain very different ideas of what is prudent.

The same person might have very different ideas of prudence and consequently might act very differently at different times. Indeed, a man's ideas of what is prudent in religious revivals depend, as they often should, on the state of his own feelings and on the feelings that surround him. This is because what would be prudent under some circumstances would be highly imprudent in others. What would be prudent for a man in a certain state of his feelings and under certain circumstances would be the height of imprudence in the same person under other circumstances.

In most cases, it is extremely difficult to form, and often very wrong to publicly express, an opinion condemning a measure as imprudent—a measure that is not condemned by the Word of God—without fully knowing the feelings and circumstances of the individual and people at the time the measure was adopted. If Christians and ministers would keep these things in mind, a great many uncharitable and critical speeches would be avoided, and much injury to the cause of truth and righteousness would be prevented.

6. *You can see why sinners and lukewarm Christians are not disturbed by dull preaching or praying.* It does not take hold of their feelings at all and therefore does not distress or offend them. Hence, we see that, in a religious revival in which cold and wicked hearts are disturbed with plain and pungent preaching, if a dull minister is called upon and preaches to the people, the wicked and coldhearted will praise his preaching. This shows why, in seasons of revival, we often hear sinners and lukewarm Christians wish that their minister would preach as he used to, that he would be himself again. The reason for this is obvious: he did not move their hearts before, but now his fire, his spirit, and his pungency annoy them and disturb their carnal slumbers.

7. *You can see why churches are sometimes convulsed by revivals of religion.* In most churches, there are probably some hypocrites who, when revivals become highly spiritual, are disturbed by the fire and spirit of them. They inwardly and sometimes openly oppose such revivals. But when only part of the real Christians in a church awake from their slumbers and become very spiritual and heavenly, and the rest remain carnal and earthly in their outlook, the church is in danger of being torn in two. Those who are awake become more zealous, more spiritual and active, while the others, if they will not awake, will be jealous and offended and will feel rebuked by the zeal of the others.

The almost certain consequence of this will be that these two groups will no longer walk together because they do not agree. This state of feeling in a church calls for great heart-searching among all its members. And although it is to be dreaded and deeply lamented when it exists, it is easily accounted for when we look closely at our human nature. This is what sometimes will happen in spite of the attempts of men and angels to prevent it.

8. *It can be seen from this subject why ministers are sometimes unsettled by revivals.* Sometimes, without any imprudence on the part of the minister, many of his congregation will not enter into the spirit of a revival. If his own feelings become enkindled and if he feels very much for his flock and for the honor of his Master, he will most assuredly press them with truth and annoy them by his pungency and fire, until he offends them. If they feel they are wrong when he more powerfully and irresistibly forces truth upon them, then, unless their feelings alter, he will offend them even more, and perhaps in the end will find it best to leave them. All this may be as right and necessary in a minister as it was for Paul to leave places and people when their hearts were hardened and they contradicted, blasphemed, and spoke evil before the multitude. (See Acts 19:1–9, for example.)

Another case may occur in which the church may awake but the shepherd does not awake. This will inevitably alienate the congregation's affections from him and destroy their confidence in him. In either of these cases, the minister and congregation may find themselves unable to walk together, because they do not agree. In the former case, the minister may obey the command of Christ and *"shake off the dust under* [his] *feet as a testimony against them"* (Mark 6:11). In the latter, the congregation shakes off their sleepy minister; they are better without him than with him.

> "Woe to the shepherds of Israel who feed themselves! Should not the shepherds feed the flocks?...You do not feed the flock."... Therefore, O shepherds, hear the word of the LORD! Thus says the Lord GOD: "Behold, I am against the shepherds, and I

will require My flock at their hand; I will cause them to cease
feeding the sheep, and the shepherds shall feed themselves no
more; for I will deliver My flock from their mouths, that they
may no longer be food for them."   (Ezekiel 34:2–3, 9–10)

9. *It can be seen why sinners and carnal Christians have no diffi-*
culty with their most primitive emotions. It is not uncommon in revivals to hear a great deal of opposition made to what is called "animal
feeling." This kind of emotion is sometimes excited in revivals. It
is not strange or even impossible that real religious emotions are
often excited to a considerable degree when the animal feelings are
affected. It is obviously absurd to object to a revival on this account.

But in most cases, it is not the animal feelings that can give
offense, for as far as these feelings are concerned, there is a perfect
harmony of feeling between saints and sinners, between carnal and
spiritual Christians. Sinners have as much animal feeling as saints
do. Those whose faith has grown cold have as much animal feeling
as warm and spiritual Christians have. Everyone can sympathize
with natural, human emotions.

Preaching or exhortation that is calculated to awaken mere
sympathy and animal feeling can bring a perfect harmony of feeling among cold- and warmhearted Christians and sinners alike.
Everyone weeps and seems to melt. However, in this case, no one
is offended, and no one is convicted or converted. But when they
hear preaching that is spiritual, holy, ardent, and powerful, and
that directly appeals to the conscience and the heart, their tears
will soon be dried; the carnal and coldhearted will become uneasy,
and soon they will find themselves offended. As far as animal feeling goes, these groups all walk together, for in this they agree. But
as soon as feeling becomes spiritual and holy, they can go together
no farther, for here, where sinners remain impenitent and cold
hearts remain cold, they cannot agree with those who are warm
and repentant.

10. *It can be seen why impenitent sinners cannot like pure revivals of religion.* It is because God is in these revivals. They hate God, and this is the reason why God commands them to make themselves a new heart. (See Ezekiel 18:31.) This is the reason, and the only reason, why sinners need a new heart. Now, while they are under the influence of a *"carnal mind* [which] *is enmity against God"* (Romans 8:7), they hate everything that is like God to the exact degree that it bears His image. Hence, we see that the more a revival is stripped of animal feelings and of everything wrong, the more it will necessarily offend wrong hearts. The more of God, and the less of human imperfection, that can be seen in revivals, the more they will excite the enmity of carnal hearts.

11. *You can see how to view apparent revivals where there is no opposition from the wicked.* If people under the dominion of a carnal mind do not oppose a revival, it must be owing to one of three causes: either (1) they are so convicted that they dare not openly oppose, even though they are opposed in their hearts; (2) there is nothing of the Holy Spirit in the revival; or (3) the operations of the Holy Spirit are kept out of the sinner's view and covered up in the rubbish of animal feeling. Anything that keeps the work of the Holy Spirit out of the sinner's view tends to prevent opposition, and everything that exposes the hand of God to the sinner's view will certainly excite the opposition of his unregenerate heart. Therefore, whatever excitement does not call out the opposition of the wicked and wronghearted is either not a revival of religion at all or is so conducted that sinners do not see the finger of God in it.

Hence, the purer and holier the means that are used to promote a revival of religion, the more they are stripped of human weakness and sympathy, and the more like God they are, so much more will they excite the opposition of all wrong hearts. While a man's heart is wrong regarding any subject, he cannot heartily approve of what is right concerning that subject, for this would involve a contradiction. Therefore, all other things being equal, those means and preaching that call forth most of the native enmity of the heart and that are most against wrong hearts, are nearest right. This is not to say that preaching should be designed to offend people; the Gospel ought not to be preached in a manner that is highly objectionable and may justly offend someone. All such things are to be condemned. However, I still insist that holy things are offensive to unholy hearts, and while hearts remain unholy, they cannot be pleased with anything that is not unholy like themselves.

Therefore, if a sinner who is under the dominion of a *"carnal mind* [which] *is enmity against God"* (Romans 8:7) is pleased with someone's preaching, it must be either because the character of God is not faithfully expounded or the sinner is prevented from understanding it in its true light. He may be inattentive to the sermon, or he may be so taken up with the delivery that he overlooks the offensiveness of the matter. If, therefore, the words of the preaching are right and the sinner is pleased, there is something defective in the delivery. Either a lack of sincerity or something else prevents the sinner from seeing what the preaching ought to show him: that he hates God and His truth.

Hence, we see the folly of those ministers and other Christians who attempt to please people whose feelings are in a wrong state in regard to religious subjects. Sinners cannot be pleased with anything right and holy while their hearts are in this wrong state, for this would involve a contradiction.

This shows why so much wrong feeling is often stirred up in revivals of religion. Wherever the Holy Spirit comes or is seen to operate, the opposite spirit is automatically disturbed. A great degree of right and holy feelings among saints will naturally stir up a great degree of unholy and wicked feelings in all those hearts that are inflexibly wrong. The more right and holy feelings there are, the more wrong and unholy feelings there will be, unless sinners and carnal Christians bow and submit. They cannot walk together because they do not agree. The more holy and heavenly the saints become in their inclinations and conduct, the farther apart they will be from the sinners, until the light of eternity will set them as far apart as heaven and hell.

This demonstrates, beyond all contradiction, that sinners cannot be saved unless they are born again. In other words, it is plainly impossible, in the nature of things, that sinners should walk with saints and holy angels without an entire change in their hearts. As soon as the saints cease to walk *according to the course of this world"* (Ephesians 2:2), sinners think it strange that the saints *"run not with them to the same excess of riot, speaking evil of* [them]" (1 Peter 4:4 kjv). As soon as Christians awake and become spiritual and zealous, holy and heavenly, and break off from their vain and wicked associations with the world, sinners are distressed and offended. They try to imagine that it is something wrong in the saints, and in revivals, that offends them.

But the truth is, they are most offended by the little that is right in the saints, and by what most reveals God in revivals. If the saints were as holy as angels are, or as holy as they will be in heaven, sinners would, of course, be even farther from having any commonality of feeling with them. And as saints rise in holiness and sinners sink in sin, they will go farther and farther apart forever and ever.

12. *Lastly, this shows why the lives and preaching of the prophets, of Christ and His apostles, and of the revivals of the early ages of the church met with so much more violent opposition from carnal Christians and from ungodly sinners than is aimed at preachers and revivals today.* Of course, the saints in those days

> had trial of mockings and scourgings, yes, and of chains and imprisonment. They were stoned, they were sawn in two, were

> *tempted, were slain with the sword. They wandered about in*
> *sheepskins and goatskins, being destitute, afflicted, tormented;*
> *of whom the world was not worthy. They wandered in deserts*
> *and mountains, in dens and caves of the earth.*
>
> (Hebrews 11:36–38)

It cannot be denied that the preaching of the prophets, of Christ and His apostles, and of ministers in the early church was opposed with great bitterness by many professed saints and by multitudes of ungodly sinners, more than that of any preachers of the present day. Nor is it to be concealed that those who claimed to be religious were often leaders in this opposition. They stirred up the Romans to crucify Jesus, and afterward to persecute and destroy His saints and crucify His apostles. The religious leaders even endeavored to prejudice the multitude against the Savior and to prevent their listening to His discourses. *"He has a demon and is mad. Why do you listen to Him?"* (John 10:20), they said.

These same religious leaders led the way in opposing the apostles in the revivals in which they were engaged. We must admit that those revivals made a great deal of noise in the world, insomuch that the apostles were accused of turning the world *"upside down"* (Acts 17:6) and that sinners were often greatly hardened by the preaching of Christ and His apostles. Sinners *"were filled with wrath"* (Luke 4:28) and so much bitterness that Christ told His apostles to *"let them alone"* (Matthew 15:14). In some places where the apostles preached, *"some were [so] hardened"* (Acts 19:9) that they *"did not believe, but spoke evil of the Way"* (verse 9). In some cases, the apostles were forced to leave and go to other places, and sometimes to leave under very humiliating circumstances, barely escaping with their lives.

Now these are facts that we should not be embarrassed about; they are easily accounted for. All these things afford no evidence that the prophets, Christ, or His apostles were imprudent and unholy men; that their preaching was too overbearing and severe; or that there was something wrong in the management of revivals in those days. The fact is, the prophets were so much holier and so much bolder and more faithful in delivering their messages; Christ was so much more searching, plain, pungent, and personal in His preaching, and so entirely *"separate from sinners"* (Hebrews 7:26) in His life; and the apostles were so pungent and plain in their dealings with sinners and professed saints, and so self-denying and holy, that carnal Christians and ungodly sinners could not walk with them.

The means that were then used to promote revivals were holier and freer from being mixed with worldliness than they now are. There was less of that hypocritical suavity of manner and those embellishments of language that are designed to court the applause of the ungodly. Having *"renounced the hidden things of shame, not walking in craftiness nor handling the word of God deceitfully"* (2 Corinthians 4:2), they preached, *"not with persuasive words of human wisdom"* (1 Corinthians 2:4) but with *"great plainness of speech"* (2 Corinthians 3:12 KJV), so that the ungodly both in the church and outside of it were filled with wrath.

Stephen was so holy and searching in his address that the elders of Israel *"gnashed at him with their teeth"* (Acts 7:54). But this is no evidence that he was imprudent. The fact that the revivals of the present day are so much more silent and gradual in their progress than they were on the Day of Pentecost, and at many other times and places, and that they create much less noise and opposition among coldhearted Christians and ungodly sinners, does not prove that the theory of revivals is better understood now than it was then. Nor does it show that ministers and Christians who are engaged in these revivals are more prudent than the apostles and early Christians were. To support this would reveal great spiritual pride in us.

We are not to say that the human heart has changed or that the character of God has become less offensive to *"the carnal mind"* (Romans 8:7). No, the fact is, the prophets, Christ, His apostles, and the early saints were holier, bolder, more zealous, plainer, and more pungent in their preaching and were less conformed to this crazy world. In a word, they were more prudent and more like heaven than we are. This is why they were more hated than we are, why their preaching and praying gave so much more offense than ours does. In their day, revivals were freer from carnal policy and the management that tends to keep hidden the naked hand of God. This is why they made so much more noise than the revivals that we witness today, and stirred up so much of earth and hell to oppose them that they convulsed and turned the world *"upside down"* (Acts 17:6).

It was known then that men could not *"serve God and mammon"* (Matthew 6:24). It was seen to be true that *"all who desire to live godly in Christ Jesus will suffer persecution"* (2 Timothy 3:12). It was understood then that if ministers pleased men, they were not the servants of Christ. (See Galatians 1:10.) The church and world could not walk together, for they were not in agreement. Let us not be too confident and imagine that we are prudent and wise and have learned how to manage carnal Christians and sinners, whose *"carnal mind is enmity against God"* (Romans 8:7). We still must call forth their opposition to truth and holiness, as Christ and His apostles did. But if they have less difficulty with us and with our lives and preaching than they had with Christ and His apostles, it is because we are less holy, less heavenly, less like God than they were. If we walk with the lukewarm and ungodly, or they with us, it is because we agree, for two cannot walk together *"unless they are agreed."*

Nine

Stewardship

Give an account of your stewardship.
—Luke 16:2

A steward is one who is employed to transact the business of another, as his agent or representative in the business in which he is employed. His duty is to promote, in the best possible manner, the interest of his employer. He is liable at any time to be called to account for the manner in which he has transacted his business, and he may be removed at any time from his office at the pleasure of his employer.

One important aim of the parable from which our text verse comes is to teach that all men are God's stewards. The Bible declares that the silver and the gold are God's (Haggai 2:8), and that He is, in the highest possible sense, the Proprietor of the universe. Men are mere stewards, employed by God for the transaction of His business and required to do all they do for His glory. Even their eating and drinking are to be done for His glory (1 Corinthians 10:31), so that they may be strengthened for the best performance of His business.

That men are God's stewards is evident from the fact that God treats them as such. He removes them at His pleasure and disposes of the property in their hands, which He could not do if He considered them as owners of the property and not mere agents. Let me go into further detail here.

The Use of Your Time

If men are God's stewards, they are bound to give an account to Him of their time. God has created them and keeps them alive, and their time is His. If you employed someone and paid him for his time, would you not expect him to use that time in your service? Would you not consider it fraud and dishonesty for him, while on your payroll, to spend his time in idleness or in promoting his private interests? If he were often idle, that would be bad enough. But suppose that he wholly neglected your business. Would you not think that his idleness, which has caused your business to suffer, was great wickedness, for which he deserved to be punished?

Now, reader, you are God's steward. If you are an impenitent sinner, you have wholly neglected God's business and have remained idle in His vineyard, or you have been only attending to your own private interests. Are you ready to report what you have done? Are you not deceitful for neglecting the business of your Employer and for going about your own private business, to the neglect of all that justice, duty, and God require of you?

Suppose your employee used his time to oppose your interests, using your capital and time in directly opposing the business for which he was employed. Would you not consider this great dishonesty? Would you not think it very ridiculous for him to call himself an honest man? Would you not suppose yourself obliged to ask him to account for his behavior? And would you not consider anyone a villain who approved such conduct? Would you not think yourself bound to expose him publicly, so that the world might know his character, and that you might clear yourself from the charge of employing such a person?

How, then, will God view you if you use your time in opposing His interests and use His capital to directly oppose the business for which He has employed you? Are you not ashamed, then, to call yourself an honest man, and will not God consider Himself obligated to call you to account for your actions? If He did not do this, would it not be proof, on His part, of His approval of your abominable wickedness? Must He not feel constrained to make you a public example, so that the universe may know how much He abhors your crimes?

The Use of Your Abilities

Stewards are also bound to give an account of their talents, by which I mean the powers of their minds. Suppose you taught a man to be your employee, supported him during the time he was studying, and paid all the expenses of his education. Then suppose that he either neglected to use his mind in your service, or he used the powers of his cultivated intellect for the promotion of his own interests. Would you not consider this as fraud and villainy? Now, God created your mind and has been paying for your education; He has trained you for His service. But you either let your mind remain in idleness, or you pervert the powers of your cultivated intellect in order to promote your own private interests, and then you ask what you have done to deserve the wrath of God! What foolishness!

But suppose your employee used his education in opposition to your interests, and used all the powers of his mind to destroy the very interests for which he was educated and which he is employed to sustain. Would you not look upon his conduct as marked with horrid guilt? And do you, sinner, employ the powers of your mind and whatever education God may have given you in opposing His interests—perverting His truth, scattering *"firebrands, arrows, and death"* (Proverbs 26:18) all around you—and think you will escape His curse? Will not the Almighty take vengeance upon such wretchedness?

The Use of Your Influence

Moreover, a steward is bound to give an account for the influence he exerts upon others around him. Suppose you employed a man, educated him until he possessed great talents, put a great sum of money into his hands, praised him highly to your friends, and placed him in circumstances to exert an immense influence in the community. Then suppose he refused or neglected to exert this influence in promoting your interests. Would you not consider this a perpetual fraud practiced upon you?

But suppose he exerted his influence against you, and even used the money you lent him to oppose your interests. What language, in your estimation, could then express your sense of his guilt?

Reader, whatever influence God has given you, if you are an impenitent sinner, you are not only neglecting to use it for God, to build up His kingdom, but you are using it in opposition to His interests and glory. For this, do you not deserve the damnation of hell? Perhaps you are rich or well educated, or maybe you have great influence in society and are refusing to use it to save the souls of men but are using it to drag all who are within the sphere of your influence down to the gates of hell. What will you say to God when He calls you to give an account of your life?

The Use of Your Possessions

You must give an account for the manner in which you use the property in your possession. Suppose your employee refused to use the money with which you entrusted him for the promotion of your interests. Or suppose he considered it his own and used it for his own private interests or applied it to the gratification of his lusts, while at the same time your business was suffering. Or suppose that this employee held the purse strings of your wealth, and

that you had multitudes of other employees whose necessities were
to be supplied out of the means in his hands. What if their welfare,
and even their lives, depended on these supplies, yet this employee
used the money to satisfy his own desires? What would you think
of such wickedness? You entrusted him with your money and
instructed him to take care of your other employees, and through
his neglect they were led to the doors of death.

Reader, God's money is in your hands, and you are surrounded
by God's children, whom He commands you to love as you do
yourself. God might, with perfect justice, have given His property
to them instead of you. The world is full of poverty, desolation, and
death. Hundreds and millions are perishing, body and soul, each
day. God calls you to exert yourself as His steward for their salvation, to use all the property in your possession in order to promote
the greatest possible amount of happiness among your fellow creatures. The Macedonian cry comes from the four winds of heaven,
"*Come over...and help us*" (Acts 16:9), yet you refuse to help. You
hoard up the wealth in your possession, live in luxury, and let your
fellowmen go to hell. What language can describe your guilt?

But suppose your employee, when you called him to give
an account, said, "Have I not acquired this property by my own
efforts?" Would you not answer, "You have used my money to do
it. You have used my time, for which I have paid you. The money
you have gained is mine"? Likewise, when God calls upon you to
use the property in your possession for Him, do you say it is yours,
that you have obtained it by your own efforts? I ask you, whose
time have you used, and whose talents and means? Did not God
create you? Has He not sustained you? Has He not prospered you
and given you all His success? Yes; your time is His, your all is
His, and you have no right to say the wealth you have is yours. It is
His, and you are bound to use it for His glory. Don't you see that
God would do wrong not to call you to account and punish you for

filling your pockets with His money and calling it your own? If you are doing this, don't call yourself a Christian.

The Use of Your Soul

You must give an account for your soul. You have no right to go to hell. God has a right to your soul, and your going to hell would injure the whole universe. It would injure hell, because it would increase its torments. It would injure heaven, because it would deprive it of your services. Who will take your place in singing praises to God? Who will contribute your share to the happiness of heaven?

Suppose you had an employee to whom you had given life, whom you had educated at great expense, and who willfully threw that life away. Does he have a right to dispose of a life that has so much value to you? God has made your soul, sustained you, and educated you, so that you are now able to serve and glorify Him forever. Do you have the right to go to hell, to throw away your soul, and thus to rob God of your service? Do you have the right to make hell more miserable and heaven less happy, and thus injure God and all the universe?

Do you still say, "What if I do lose my soul? It is nobody's business but my own"? That is false; it is everybody's business. A man might just as well bring a contagious disease into a city, spread dismay and death all around, and say it was nobody's business but his own.

The Souls of Others

You must give an account for the souls of others. God commands you to be a coworker with Him in converting the world. He needs your services, for He saves souls only through the help of people like you. If souls are lost, or if the Gospel is not spread over the world, sinners put all the blame upon Christians, as if they are the only ones bound to be active in the cause of Christ, to exercise benevolence, to pray for a lost world, to pull sinners out of the fire. I wonder, who has absolved you from these duties? Instead of doing your duty, you lie as a stumbling block in the way of other sinners. Thus, instead of helping to save a world, all your actions help to send souls to hell.

The Ideas You Promote

You are bound to give an account of the ideas you entertain and propagate. God's kingdom is to be built up by truth, not by error. Your ideas will have an important bearing upon the influence you exert over those around you.

Suppose your business required your employees to have right ideas concerning the manner of doing it and the principles involved in it. And suppose you had given your employees, in writing, a set of rules in relation to all the affairs with which they were entrusted. Then, if they neglected to examine those rules, if they perverted their meaning—and therefore perverted their own conduct—if they were instrumental in deceiving others and leading them in the way of disobedience, would you not consider this as criminal behavior, deserving the severest condemnation?

God has given you rules for your conduct. The Bible is a plain revelation of His will in relation to all your actions. Do you neglect or pervert it? Do you go astray yourself and lead others with you in the way of disobedience and death, and then call yourself an honest man? How shameful!

Your Opportunities to Serve God

You must give an account of your opportunities for doing good. If you employ a man to transact your business, you expect him to take advantage of the state of the market and of things in general, to take every opportunity to promote your interests. Suppose that, during the busy seasons of the year, he spent his time in idleness or in his own private affairs, paying no attention to the most favorable opportunities for promoting your interests. Would you not soon say to him, "*Give an account of your stewardship, for you can no longer be steward*" (Luke 16:2)?

Now, sinner, you have always neglected opportunities for serving God, for warning your fellow sinners, for promoting revivals of religion and advancing the interest of truth. You have been diligent only to promote your own private interests and have entirely neglected the interests of your great Employer. Are you not a wretch, and do you not deserve to be put out of the stewardship as a dishonest man, to be sent to the prison of the universe? How can you escape the damnation of hell?

Remarks

1. *From this subject, you can see why the business of this world is a snare that drowns men's souls in destruction and perdition.* Sinners transact business to promote their own private interests, and not as God's stewards. Thus, they act dishonestly, defraud God, grieve the Holy Spirit, and promote their own sensuality, pride, and death. If men considered themselves as God's stewards, they would do nothing that would not please Him. God never created this world to be a snare to men; He designed it to be a delightful abode for them. But now how perverted it is, and how abused!

If all business were done unto God, people would not find it such a temptation toward fraud and dishonesty. It would have no tendency to wean their souls from God or to banish Him from their thoughts. If your gardener were very busy all day caring for your plants, consulting you on how to care for them, and doing your pleasure continually, would this have a tendency to banish you from his thoughts? No, he would always be aware of your wishes. In a similar manner, if you were busy all day seeking God's glory and transacting all your business for Him, acting as His steward, aware that His eye was upon you, always asking if this or that will please Him, your work would have no tendency to distract your mind and turn your thoughts from God.

Now, if you consider yourself as God's steward, doing His business; if you always look after His interests and His glory and consider all your possessions as His; the more busily you are engaged in His service, the more will God be present in all your thoughts.

2. *You see why idleness is a snare to the soul.* A man who is idle is dishonest, forgets his responsibility, refuses to serve God, and gives himself up to the temptations of the Devil. In fact, the idle man tempts the Devil to tempt him.

3. *You see the error of the idea that men cannot attend to business and religion at the same time.* Anyone who pleads this maxim is deceived by his own words, for no man can believe that honest employment, pursued for God's glory, is inconsistent with religion. A man's religion ought to be a part of his business. If he performs his business with right motives, his lawful and necessary business is as much a necessary part of religion as prayer, going to church, or reading his Bible. If it is true that a man cannot be religious while thus pursuing his business, if his work is wicked, he must relinquish it; and if it is honest work but is pursued in an unlawful manner, he must pursue it lawfully, or in either case he will lose his soul. But if a man's business is lawful, let him pursue it honestly with right motives, and he will find no difficulty in attending to his business and being religious at the same time. A life of business is best for Christians, for it exercises their graces and makes them strong.

4. *It is evident that most men do not consider themselves as God's stewards from the fact that they consider the losses they sustain in business as their own losses.* Suppose that many of your debtors fail to pay what they owe, and your employees speak of it as their own loss. Would you not think they are ridiculous? Is it not quite as ridiculous for you, if any of your Lord's debtors fail, to make yourself very uneasy and unhappy about it? Is it your loss or His? If you have done your duty, if you have taken suitable care of His property and a loss is sustained, it is nor your loss, but His. You should look at your sins and your duty and not be frightened. God will not become bankrupt. If you acted as God's steward, you would not think of speaking of the loss as your own loss. But if you have considered the property in your possession as your own, no wonder that God has taken it out of your hands.

5. *You see that it is ridiculous to refer to some institutions in the world as charitable institutions.* Institutions for the promotion of religion are the charities of God, not of man. The funds are God's, and it is His requirement that they be spent according to His directions. God, then, is the giver, and not men; and to consider the charities as the gift of men is to maintain that the funds belong to men and not to God. To call them charitable institutions, in the sense in which they are usually spoken of, is to say that men are doing God a favor by giving Him their money, and that they consider Him as an object of charity. If you were to instruct an employee to give a certain amount of funds for the benefit of the poor in a certain community, this would be charity in you but not in him. It would be ridiculous for him to pretend that the charity was his.

What do you think of yourself when you talk of supporting these charitable institutions as if God, the owner of the universe, were soliciting charity and His servants were agents of an infinite beggar? How amazing it is that God does not take presumptuous men and put them in hell in a moment, and then with the money in their hands execute His plans for converting the world!

It is no less ridiculous for people to suppose that, by giving the money in their hands toward world missions, they are being charitable toward others, for the money is not theirs. They are God's stewards, and they only give God's money back to Him.

6. *When the servants of the Lord come to your door telling you to give some of the money in your possession to His treasury, to defray the expenses of His government and kingdom, why do you call it your own and say you can't spare it?* What do you mean by calling the agents beggars and saying you are sick of seeing so many beggars—that you are disgusted with those agents of charitable institutions? Suppose one of your employees under such circumstances were to call your clients beggars and say he was sick of so many beggars. Would you not call him to give an account, and let him see that the property in his possession was yours, not his?

7. *You see the great wickedness of hoarding up property during one's lifetime and leaving a part of it to the church when one dies.* What a will, to leave God half of His own property! Suppose a servant were to make a will, leaving to his master part of his own property! Yet this is called piety. Do you think that Christ will always be a beggar? And yet the church is greatly overconfident with its great charitable donations and legacies to Jesus Christ.

8. *Impenitent sinners will be finally and eternally disgraced.* Do you not consider it a disgrace to a man when he is convicted of fraud in transacting the business of his employer? Is not such a man deservedly thrown out of the business? Is he not a disgrace to himself and his family? Can anybody trust him? How, then, will you appear before an injured God and an injured universe—a God whose laws and rights you have despised, a universe with whose interests you have been at war? In the solemn Judgment, you will be disgraced, your name will be detested, and you will become the

contempt of hell itself because of the innumerable frauds and villainies you have practiced upon God and upon His creatures!

But perhaps you are one who claims to be religious. Will your claim cover up your selfishness and vile hypocrisy, while you have defrauded God, spent His money upon your lusts, and called them beggars who came telling you to pay what you owe to God's treasury? How will you hold up your head in the face of heaven? How dare you now pray? How dare you sit at the Communion table? How dare you claim to have the religion of Jesus Christ if you do not consider all that you have as His and use it all for His glory?

9. *We have here a true test of Christian character.* True Christians consider themselves as God's stewards. They act for Him, live for Him, transact business for Him, eat and drink for His glory, live and die to please Him. But sinners and hypocrites live for themselves. They consider their time, their talents, their influence as their own, and they use them all for their own private interests and thus drown themselves in destruction and perdition.

We are informed that, on Judgment Day, Christ will say to each one who is accepted, *"Well done, good and faithful servant"* (Matthew 25:21). Reader, could He truly say this of you: *"Well done, good and faithful servant; you were faithful over a few things"* (verse 21), that is, over the things committed to your charge? He will pronounce no false judgment, put no false estimate upon things, and if He cannot say this truthfully, you will not be accepted but will be thrown down to hell.

Now, reader, what is your character, and what has been your conduct? God will soon call you to give an account of your stewardship. Have you been faithful to God, faithful to your own soul and the souls of others? Are you ready to have your accounts examined, your conduct scrutinized, and your life weighed according to God's standard of measurement? Do you have a share in the blood of Jesus Christ? If not, repent. Repent now of all your wickedness, and *"lay hold of the hope set before* [you]" (Hebrews 6:18). Listen! A voice cries in your ear, *"Give an account of your stewardship, for you can no longer be steward"* (Luke 16:2).

Ten

The Doctrine of Election

Just as He chose us in Him before the foundation of the
world, that we should be holy and without blame before Him
in love, having predestined us to adoption as sons by Jesus
Christ to Himself, according to the good pleasure of His will.
—Ephesians 1:4–5

Many people are opposed to the doctrine of election and try to explain it away. Either they misunderstand it or they make unsubstantiated inferences from it. They suppose it to mean that the elect will be saved no matter what their conduct may be. But the doctrine of election does not mean that part of mankind is to be saved irrespective of their moral character or their conduct.

The understanding that some people have is that the doctrine of election is an encouragement to the elect to persevere in sin because they know that their salvation is sure. They also infer from the doctrine that there is no possibility of salvation for the non-elect. This inference would drive the non-elect to desperation, on the ground any efforts they make to be saved will be of no avail. But both this interpretation of the doctrine and this inference are false. This doctrine does not prove that the non-elect are created for damnation and cannot be saved no matter what they do. Election does not secure the salvation of the elect regardless of their character and conduct, nor does it throw any obstacle in the way of the salvation of the non-elect.

The doctrine of election does not mean that the elect have any particular provision in the Atonement for their salvation, more

192

than for the non-elect. It does not imply that the unconverted elect are any better than the non-elect, nor does it imply that the unconverted elect are any more beloved by God than the non-elect. Even so, the doctrine of election does mean that a part of the human race is chosen for eternal salvation. They are not only chosen as a whole, but also as individuals, every one of whom will finally be saved.

This doctrine is taught in the Bible. It is clearly shown in the Scripture that begins this chapter. Peter directed his first epistle…

> *to the pilgrims of the Dispersion in Pontus, Galatia, Cappadocia, Asia, and Bithynia, elect according to the foreknowledge of God the Father, in sanctification of the Spirit, for obedience and sprinkling of the blood of Jesus Christ: Grace to you and peace be multiplied. Blessed be the God and Father of our Lord Jesus Christ, who according to His abundant mercy has begotten us again to a living hope through the resurrection of Jesus Christ from the dead, to an inheritance incorruptible and undefiled and that does not fade away, reserved in heaven for you, who are kept by the power of God through faith for salvation ready to be revealed in the last time.* (1 Peter 1:1–5)

In 2 Timothy 1:9, the apostle Paul wrote,

> *[God] has saved us and called us with a holy calling, not according to our works, but according to His own purpose and grace which was given to us in Christ Jesus before time began.*

Much effort has been put forth to explain these passages so as to show that they do not teach election as I have stated it. But all of the attempts to explain this doctrine away have uniformly been abandoned, which fully demonstrates that the doctrine stands and cannot be explained away: a part of mankind is chosen for eternal life and salvation.

God must have foreknown who would and who would not be saved. He must have had a perfect knowledge of it from the beginning. Peter asserted the foreknowledge of God by address-ing Christians as *"elect according to the foreknowledge of God"* (1 Peter 1:2). Paul, in the eighth chapter of his epistle to the Romans, said,

> *For whom He foreknew, He also predestined to be conformed to the image of His Son, that He might be the firstborn among many brethren. Moreover whom He predestined, these He also called; whom He called, these He also justified; and whom He justified, these He also glorified.*
>
> (Romans 8:29–30)

If God foreknew whom He would save, He must have had a specific purpose concerning it. It is unreasonable to suppose that He either did not want to save them or had no intention of doing so, for God *"desires all men to be saved"* (1 Timothy 2:4). He must therefore have had the intention that they should be saved.

The doctrine of election may be inferred from the fact that, with God, there is no past or future time, but all eternity is pres-ent time to Him. The beginning and the end of time, all the events of time and eternity, the Judgment Day and eternity beyond, are present to His mind. The name and character and eternal destiny of every creature are present to Him, and it is a very wrong view of God that exhibits Him as having no definite plan in relation to all the concerns of His vast empire. Indeed, it is virtually denying God and robbing Him of the essential attributes of His nature.

If God does not know the individuals who will be saved, it is impossible for Him to know that any will be saved. If He has planned to save His saints as a body, he must have designed to save them as individuals, for the body is made up of individuals.

Why Christians Are Elected

Now, why are Christians elected? It is not because the elect are any better by nature than others. Paul said, "[We are called] *with a holy calling, not according to our works, but according to His own purpose and grace which was given to us in Christ Jesus before time began*" (2 Timothy 1:9). Nor does God more strongly desire the salvation of the elect than of the non-elect. Christ did not feel any particular partiality for the elect more than for the non-elect. (See 1 Timothy 2:3–4.) In short, it was nothing in the nature or character of men that led Him to make this distinction and to choose some over others.

Election is not partial, which means that there is no undue bias or favor toward one individual or party. It does not depend upon anything in the character of the elect, or upon any particular prejudice or partiality that God has in their favor. The question of their election did not depend upon anything in them, but upon the best interests of God's government. In electing them, God did not look over the human family to see whom He loved best, but upon whom, in the wisest administration of His government, He could morally influence enough to save them. It was no partiality to them, but a high and holy regard for the great interests of His immense kingdom that led to their election.

God must have had some good and substantial reason for choosing one man over another. Some say that election means that God acted arbitrarily. But my understanding of the doctrine of election is much different. For although God has not told us why He has selected one instead of another, He has told us certain things from which we may justly infer the reasons that led Him to this selection. The Scriptures inform us that God is good, infinitely good, and that He does good. From the fact that He is infinitely good, we are bound to infer that He does all the good He can.

Moreover, He asks, "*What more could have been done to My vineyard that I have not done in it?*" (Isaiah 5:4). If God does not save all men, it must be because all cannot consistently be saved, and because the salvation of all men would require such a change in the administration of His government that it would do more hurt than good in the universe. If the salvation of all men would be most for the glory of God and for the best interests of His kingdom, then all men would be saved.

The fact is, the conversion of all men would require a very different arrangement and administration of the divine government from that which we now experience. It would have to have sufficient moral influence upon this world to turn all men to God. Also, this change in the administration of the divine government might in many ways so disarrange the concerns of the universe that more harm would be done than good. Therefore, if any part of mankind is saved, it is because God can wisely save them.

The elect, then, must be those whom God foresaw could be converted under the wisest administration of His government. He foresaw that certain individuals could, with this wisest amount of moral influence, be reclaimed and sanctified, and for this reason they were chosen for eternal life. This does not mean that God foresaw that some men would be better by nature than others, and that on this account they could be more easily turned to God. Rather, He saw that they would be sufficiently influenced by moral principles that their opposition would be subdued and their souls would be saved.

There is no injustice in this. God was under obligation to no one; He might in perfect justice have sent all mankind to hell. The doctrine of election will damn no one: by giving the non-elect what they deserve, God does them no injustice, and surely His exercising grace in the salvation of the elect is no act of injustice to the non-elect. This is especially true if we take into consideration the fact that the only reason why the non-elect will not be saved is that they stubbornly refuse salvation. God offers mercy to all. The Atonement is sufficient for all. All may come and are under an obligation to be saved. God strongly desires their salvation and does all that He wisely can to save them. Why, then, should the doctrine of election be thought unjust?

Election poses no obstacle to the salvation of the non-elect. The election of some to eternal life, on the ground that they can be converted under the wisest administration of God's government, is by no means an obstacle to the conversion of the non-elect. God uses all the means that are consistent with wisdom to reclaim and save them, too. The conversion of the elect, instead of being an obstacle, is a powerful persuasion to the non-elect to turn and live. Because of the relations that the elect have to the multitudes of the non-elect, the conversion of the elect is among the most powerful motivations that could be presented for the conversion of the non-elect.

Some may ask, "Why does God use means with the non-elect when He is certain they will not accept?" It is because He intends that they will be without excuse. (See Romans 1:20.) God will demonstrate His willingness and their obstinacy before the universe. He will rid His garments of their blood; and although He knows that their rejection of the offer will only enhance their guilt and aggravate their deep damnation, still He will make the offer, as there is no other way in which to illustrate His infinite willingness to save them and their perverse rejection of His grace.

This is the best that could be done for the inhabitants of this world. It is reasonable to infer from the infinite benevolence of God that the plan of His government includes the salvation of a greater number than could have been saved under any other mode of administration. To suppose that God would prefer a mode of administration that would save fewer people, would be to accuse

Him of a lack of benevolence. It is undoubtedly true that He could vary the course of events in order to save other individuals than He does. He could convert more in one particular neighborhood, family, or nation, or at one particular time, than He does.

God has the good of His whole kingdom in mind. He works on a vast and comprehensive scale. He has no partialities for individuals, but He moves forward in the administration of His government with His eye upon the general good, intending to convert the greatest number and produce the greatest amount of happiness within His kingdom.

When Election Takes Place

The apostle said that election occurred before the world began, or from eternity. This must have been when the plan of the divine government was settled in God's mind, and the present mode of administration was decided upon. Some suppose that men are not elected until they are converted, and so they confuse election with conversion. But this is neither reasonable nor scriptural. Christ will say to His saints on Judgment Day, *"Come, you blessed of My Father, inherit the kingdom prepared for you from the foundation of the world"* (Matthew 25:34). And certainly it is unreasonable to suppose that an unchangeable God has changed His mind in regard to an individual, has made a new choice, and has elected him to eternal life when He sees that he is converted.

Moreover, election does not supersede the necessity of means for the conversion of the elect. They are chosen for salvation through the sanctification of the Spirit and belief in the truth. They must then hear, believe, and obey the truth. If the end is to be accomplished, the necessary means must be used. If a farmer knew that God had decided beforehand whether he would have a crop or not, would he say to himself, "If I am meant to have a crop, I'll have it, whether I sow my land or not"? Would a sick man neglect to use medicine because he knows that God has numbered his days and already decided whether he would die or not? Certainly not. If the farmer is to have a crop, he must sow his field and use the necessary means. If the sick man is to live, he must drink the medicine. Likewise, if the means of salvation are not used, not even the elect can be saved, and those who neglect the means will never make their *"calling and election sure"* (2 Peter 1:10 KJV).

This view of the subject allows no room for presumption on the one hand, nor for despair on the other. No one can justly say, "If I am to be saved, I will be saved, no matter what I do." Nor can anyone say, "If I am to be damned, I will be damned, no matter what I do." Sinners, your salvation or damnation is as absolutely dependent upon your own choice as if God neither knew or foreordained anything about it.

It may be known who are elected. Those of the elect who are already converted are known by their character and conduct. They demonstrate the reality of their election by their obedience to God. Those who are unconverted may settle the question, each one for himself, whether he is elected or not, in order to have satisfactory proof whether he is of that happy number. If you will now submit yourselves to God, you may know that you are elected. But every hour you put off submission increases the evidence that you are not elected.

Remarks

1. *Knowing that "the carnal mind is enmity against God" (Romans 8:7), that men are utterly opposed to the way of salvation, that they hate the Gospel and all the efforts that are made to save them, what encouragement would I have to preach the Gospel, were it not that I know that God has chosen some for eternal life and that many or all my hearers may be of this number?* God in His providence has a

plan to reach many with the arrows of His truth. It is this consideration alone that encourages me and other ministers to hold forth the Word of Life so that others can hear it.

2. *This doctrine provides no foundation for a controversy with God.* Rather, it lays a broad foundation for gratitude on the part of both the elect and the non-elect. The elect certainly have great cause to be thankful that they are thus distinguished. What a thought, to have your name written in the Book of Life, to be chosen by God as an heir of eternal salvation, to be adopted into His family, to be destined to enjoy His presence, and to bathe your soul in the boundless ocean of His love forever and ever! But the non-elect also have obligations to be thankful. You ought to be grateful if any of your fellowmen are saved. If all were lost, God would be just. And if any of your neighbors or friends, or any of this dying world receive the gift of eternal life, you ought to be grateful and render everlasting thanks to God.

3. *Foreknowledge and election are not inconsistent with free agency but are founded upon it.* The elect were chosen for eternal life because God foresaw that, in perfect exercise of their freedom, they could be moved to repent and embrace the Gospel. Election does not mean that people will be forced to go to heaven against their will.

The perversion and abuse of this doctrine forcibly illustrate the madness of the human heart and its utter opposition to the terms of salvation. The fact that God foreknows and has plans in regard to every other event of life is not an excuse for remaining idle or indifferent on these subjects. But where their duty to God is concerned, and here alone, sinners seize the Scriptures and use them to their own destruction. This fact proves that sinners want an excuse for disobeying God, that they desire a justification for living in sin, and that they seek an occasion for making war upon their Maker.

4. *The non-elect often enjoy as great or greater privileges than the elect.* Many men have lived and died under the sound of the Gospel, have seen all the means of salvation during a long life, but have died in their sins. Meanwhile, others have been converted upon their first hearing of the Gospel of God. Yet this difference is not owing to the fact that the elect always have more of the strivings of the Spirit than the non-elect. Many who die in their sins appear to have had conviction for a great part of their lives; have often been deeply impressed with a sense of their sins and the value of their souls, but have strongly entrenched themselves under a *"refuge of lies"* (Isaiah 28:17); have loved the world and hated God; have fought their way through all the obstacles that were thrown around them to hedge up their way to death; and have literally forced their own passage to the gates of hell.

5. *The doctrine of election is often a stumbling block to sinners.* But why should it be? God's purposes and plans are settled and have as absolute an influence in religion as they do in anything else. God certainly designed the day and circumstances of your death as much as He planned whether your soul will be saved. The doctrine of election is not only expressly declared in the Bible, but is plainly a reasonable doctrine.

Suppose your neighbor is sick, and when you visit him you find out that he will neither eat nor drink, and that he is nearly starving to death. When you have questioned him further, he calmly replies that he believes in the sovereignty of God, that his days are numbered, that the time and circumstances of his death are settled, that he cannot die before his time, and that all the efforts he could make would not enable him to live a moment beyond his time. When you attempt to argue against him, he accuses you of being a heretic, of not believing in divine sovereignty. Now, if you were to see a man reasoning and acting thus on worldly subjects, you would call him crazy. If farmers, mechanics, and merchants were to reason in this way in regard to their worldly business, they would be considered fit subjects for the insane asylum.

6. *The question of your salvation is open for your decision.* You are left to exercise your freedom as much as if God neither knew nor planned anything in regard to your salvation. Allow me to illustrate this. Suppose there is a great famine in your town and that John Jacob Astor has food in great abundance. Imagine he is a benevolent and liberal-minded man who is willing to supply the whole city with provisions free of charge. But then suppose there is a widespread and unreasonable prejudice against him, insomuch that when he advertises in the daily papers that his storehouses are open, that anyone can come and receive provisions free of charge, they all obstinately refuse to accept the offer.

Now suppose that Mr. Astor employs several young men to carry provisions around the city, stopping at every door, but still the people join together and say they would rather die than be indebted to him for food. Many have said so much against him that they are utterly ashamed to acknowledge their dependence upon him. Others are unwilling to offend those who have spoken against Mr. Astor, and the tide of public sentiment is so strong that no one has the moral courage to break loose from the multitude and accept life.

Now imagine that Mr. Astor knew beforehand the state of the public mind, that all the citizens hated him and would rather die than be indebted to him for life. Suppose he also knew from the beginning that there were certain arguments that he could present to certain individuals that would change their minds, and that he would proceed to press them with these considerations until they had given up their opposition, had most thankfully accepted his provisions, and were saved from death. Suppose he used all the arguments and means that he wisely could to persuade the rest, but despite his benevolent efforts, they stood fast and preferred death rather than submission to his proposals. Supposing that Mr. Astor had perfect knowledge from the beginning of this whole matter, would not the question of life and death still be as entirely open for the decision of every individual as if he knew nothing about it?

7. *Lastly, God requires you to be as diligent as possible to make your calling and election sure.* In choosing His elect, God has thrown the responsibility of their being saved upon them. The end result hangs upon their consent to the terms. You are all perfectly able to give your consent and this moment to lay hold of eternal life. Without your choice, no election can save you, and no reprobation can damn you.

> *The Spirit and the bride say, "Come!" And let him who hears say, "Come!" And let him who thirsts come. Whoever desires, let him take the water of life freely.*   (Revelation 22:17)

The responsibility is yours. God does all that He wisely can, and He challenges you to show what more He could do that He has not done. If you go to hell, you will go stained with your own blood. God is clear; angels are clear. Before your own Master, you stand or fall. (See Romans 14:4.) Mercy waits; the Spirit strives; Jesus stands at the door and knocks. (See Revelation 3:20.) Do not, then, pervert this doctrine and make it a stumbling block so that you end up in the depths of hell.

Eleven

Reprobation

People will call them rejected silver,
because the Lord has rejected them.
—Jeremiah 6:30

These words were spoken about a generation of Israel with whom
God had used every suitable means to reclaim and save, and who
had withstood them all and had remained obstinate and impenitent to the end. The prophet Jeremiah said to them,

> *O daughter of my people, dress in sackcloth and roll about in*
> *ashes! Make mourning as for an only son, most bitter lamen-*
> *tation; for the plunderer will suddenly come upon us.*
> (Jeremiah 6:26)

The Lord said to Jeremiah,

> *I have set you as an assayer and a fortress among My people,*
> *that you may know and test their way. They are all stubborn*
> *rebels, walking as slanderers. They are bronze and iron, they*
> *are all corrupters; the bellows blow fiercely, the lead is con-*
> *sumed by the fire; the smelter refines in vain, for the wicked*
> *are not drawn off. People will call them rejected silver, because*
> *the Lord has rejected them.* (verses 27–30)

This is a striking instance of the use of figurative language in
the Bible as the best possible means of conveying truth. Literal
language may have a variety of meanings, may be understood

differently by different individuals, and may change with the passage of time. But figurative language always remains the same, conveys the same ideas, in all ages and to all nations. Here the people of Israel were compared to metal that a refiner was trying to purify in the fire. The means that God had used to sanctify them are compared to fire, and the refiner is represented as having raised his heat to such a degree as to burn the bellows and, as it were, to consume the metal itself by the intensity of the heat. And yet he could not succeed in separating the dross from the silver. He then pronounces it reprobate, or rejected silver, fit only to be thrown away.

The house of Israel, likewise, was unreformable, and the more strenuously God pressed the means of her sanctification, the more her reprobation and obstinacy manifested itself. God therefore declared that men should call the Israelites reprobate and should understand that the Lord had rejected them.

My goal in this chapter is to discuss the doctrine of reprobation. Because the subject is so copious, I must condense what I plan to say under each of the following subheads, and content myself with giving a mere outline of this important doctrine. The subject is like a mine of gold: the deeper you go, the richer the vein.

What Is Reprobation?

First, what is the doctrine of reprobation? To reprobate a thing is to pronounce it good for nothing, rejected, cast away. The reprobate among mankind are those who are to be lost, to be cast out from the presence of God and the glory of His power forever. I do not want to prove here that any particular part of mankind will be finally lost. To attempt to prove this is unnecessary and irrelevant here. It is only necessary now to say that those who will be finally rejected and lost are the reprobates.

What Is Not the Foundation of This Doctrine

Second, what are *not* the reasons upon which this doctrine is founded? In other words, what are not the reasons that reprobates are lost?

God's Ill Will toward Man

People are not reprobate because God has any malevolent feelings to gratify or any ill will toward His creatures. He never feels malevolently toward even the most wicked beings in the universe. He blames them and feels grieved and indignant at their conduct, but He is never malevolent. God is often represented in the Bible as being angry with the wicked. These representations are just, and the Bible means as it says. He is angry, but His anger is not malevolent. He has the feelings of a good governor who sees rebels arrayed against the government, introducing disorder, and destroying public and private happiness. God feels a benevolent opposition to such conduct, a holy indignation, to a degree equal to His love of virtue and happiness. His love for the public good makes Him resolute and firm in executing the laws against the reprobates.

Their Damnation Is Required

They are not reprobate because the glory of God or the interest of the universe requires their damnation even if they repent. Some people think that the reprobation and damnation of a part of mankind is indispensable to the glory of God and the good of the universe. They have supposed that God's whole moral character could be displayed in no other way. They suppose that sin was necessary for the greatest good, and that God decreed the sins, the reprobation, and the damnation of the finally impenitent as the only way of showing before the universe the whole circle of divine attributes, and of producing the greatest amount of good.

Consequently, in their opinion, God really prefers the existence of sin to its nonexistence, rebellion to obedience, the damnation of a part of mankind to the salvation of the whole.

I consider this to be a dangerous error, highly dishonorable to God, injurious to His government, and in a high degree calculated to stir up rebellion against His throne. I do not suppose that sin is the necessary means of the greatest good, and I consider punishment necessary only because moral agents have not been, and will not be, obedient without witnessing execution of law. If all the subjects of God's government had remained obedient, a practical illustration of divine justice would have been uncalled for. If all God's subjects had continued to obey without the infliction of the penalty, it would not have been to the glory of God, but to the infinite dishonor of God, to have sent anyone to hell. Such strong measures as the infinite penalty of God's law, far from being essential to His glory, are only warrantable and appear glorious in Him when all milder means fail to procure and perpetuate obedience.

What is the use of developing the attribute of justice except to procure respect for God's authority and thereby to secure obedience? If men were obedient without this practical exhibition of justice, certainly punishment would be uncalled for. But God's glory requires that men be reprobated and damned, simply in view of the fact that they sin and persist in rebellion, not because their rebellion and damnation are preferred over their obedience and salvation.

The Atonement Is Insufficient

Men are not reprobated because of any lack of sufficiency in the Atonement. The Atonement is often wrongly represented as simply a business transaction, as if the persons in the Godhead had made a bargain in which the Son agreed to pay the Father so much suffering for so much sin committed. In other words, Christ's death was like the payment of a promissory note, the exact amount of suffering paid by the surety that was due to the guilty. Some who have maintained this idea of the Atonement—to avoid the inevitable conclusion that if the debt were literally paid for all, then all would be saved—have maintained that no atonement was made except for the elect, and the non-elect were as entirely ignored in the Atonement as the devils were.

But Christ did not agree to purchase a part of mankind from the Father by paying only so much suffering for so much sin, choosing from among men as we would from among a flock of sheep. This shows God as having sold the elect to His Son for so much, and as leaving the rest to go to hell without any chance for salvation. Neither my Bible, my intellect, my conscience, nor my heart will for one moment admit such a view of the Atonement to be true. The Atonement is a transaction that renders the salvation of every sinner possible, but is not calculated or designed to pay the debt of any sinner so as to make his salvation an act of justice. It provides for the salvation of all men, but of itself makes sure the salvation of no man. If no one had been saved, it would have reflected infinite glory on the character of God; it would have displayed, in the most striking and impressive manner, His whole heart on the subject of his law, its precepts, and its penalties. And if all men should reject it, it would still be glorious, and would throw a radiance around the scepter of His justice that would light their footsteps to the gates of hell.

Why Some People Are Reprobates

Third, why are reprobates rejected and lost? Because they are unwilling to be saved; that is, they are unwilling to be saved on the only terms upon which God can consistently save them. Ask sinners whether they are willing to be saved, and they all say yes. They may say this with perfect sincerity, as long as they can be saved upon their own terms. But when you propose to them the terms of salvation upon which the Gospel proposes to save them—when they are required to repent and believe the Gospel, to forsake their sins, and give themselves up to the service of God—they will all begin to make excuses.

Now, to accept these terms is to consent to them heartily and practically. For sinners to say that they are willing to accept salvation while they actually do not accept it, is to speak falsely. To be willing is to accept it; and the fact that they do not heartily consent to and embrace the terms of salvation is proof that they are unwilling. Yes, sinners, you reject the only terms on which you can possibly be saved. Is it not, then, an insult to God for you to pretend that you are willing? The only true reason that any of you are not Christians is that you are unwilling. You are not made unwilling by any act of God because you are a reprobate; but if you are a reprobate, it is because you are unwilling.

Perhaps you object and say, "Why does God not make us willing? Is it not because He has made us reprobate that He does not change our hearts and make us willing?" No, sinner, it is not because He has made you reprobate, but because you are so obstinate that He cannot take measures that will convert you. Here you are, waiting for God to make you willing to go to heaven, and all the while you are diligently using the means to get to hell. Yes, you exert greater diligence to get to hell than it would cost to insure your salvation if your diligence were applied with equal zeal in the service of your God. You tempt God and then turn around and ask Him why He does not make you willing!

Now, sinner, let me ask you, do you think you are a reprobate? If so, what do you think the reason is that has led the infinitely benevolent God to make you reprobate? There must be some reason. What do you suppose it is? Did you ever seriously ask yourself, "What is the reason that a wise and infinitely benevolent God has never made me willing to accept salvation?" It must be for one of the following reasons:

- ✦ He is a malevolent being and desires your damnation for its own sake.

- ✦ He cannot make you willing even if He wishes to.

- ✦ You behave in such a manner that, to His infinitely benevolent mind, it appears unwise to take a course that would bring you to repentance.

Now, which of these do you think it is? You will probably not decide that He is malevolent and desires your damnation because He delights in misery. Nor will you, I suppose, determine that He could not convert you even if He wanted to. The other, then, must be the reason, and that is that your heart, your conduct, and your stubbornness are so abominable in His sight that He sees that to try to secure your conversion would, overall, do more hurt than good to His kingdom.

Do you wonder how I can know that the reason God does not make you willing is that He sees that it would be unwise of Him to do so? It is an irresistible inference from these two facts: that He is infinitely benevolent, and that He does not actually make you willing. I do not believe that God would neglect anything that He saw to be wise and benevolent in the great matter of man's salvation. Who can believe that He can give His only begotten and well-beloved Son to die for sinners, and then neglect any other benevolent means for their salvation? No, sinner, if you are reprobate, it is because God foresaw that you would do just as you are doing, that you would be so wicked as to defeat all the efforts that He could wisely make for your salvation.

He has tried so many things with you. He has thrown you into the furnace of affliction, and when this has not softened you, He has loaded you with benefits. He has sent you His Word, He has striven by His Spirit, He has allured you by the cross, He has tried to melt you by the groanings of Calvary and has tried to drive you back from the way to death by rolling in your ears the thunders of damnation. Clouds and darkness have been all around you; the heavens have thundered over your head; divine vengeance has hung all around your horizon the portentous clouds of coming wrath. At another time, mercy has smiled upon you from above like the noonday sun, breaking through an ocean of storms.

God has laid heaven, earth, and hell before you for consideration, in order to move your stony heart. But you deafen your ears, close your eyes, harden your heart, and say, *"Cause the Holy One of Israel to cease from before us"* (Isaiah 30:11). And what is the inference from all this? How must all this end? *"People will call them rejected silver, because the* LORD *has rejected them."*

Men are not lost because of their reprobation. That is, their reprobation is not the reason why they are lost. God does not condemn them because they are reprobated, but because they are wicked. It is their own act that leads Him to send them to hell, and not His act in reprobating them. He reprobates and punishes them for their sins, because, in spite of all He could wisely do to reclaim them, they wished to remain in their sins. He always foresaw how wicked they would be and always planned to treat them accordingly.

The salvation or damnation of the reprobate is dependent on their own choices. This, sinner, is the turning point. If you choose the way of life, you will be saved; if you choose the way of sin, you will be damned.

Because we were created as moral agents under a moral government, our salvation depends upon our own choices, and salvation is impossible for us in any other way. If you are reprobated, it is because, when the choice is given you, you choose wrong and obstinately persist in it. The reason God rejects you is that you reject Him. He reprobates you because you reprobate Him. He does it because you do it, and for no other reason. Some will object

212 Sermons on Important Subjects

to this and will say that the heathen never had the offer of salvation. This is a grave mistake.

God judges men according to the light they have. The apostle Paul said, "*For as many as have sinned without law will also perish without law, and as many as have sinned in the law will be judged by the law*" (Romans 2:12). Those who have only the light of nature, if they improve and obey that light, will be saved. But Paul affirmed that the heathen do not do this. He said that they are unwilling "*to retain God in their knowledge*" (Romans 1:28), and that for this reason they have "*changed the glory of the incorruptible God into an image made like corruptible man; and birds and four-footed animals and creeping things*" (verse 23), "*so that they are without excuse*" (verse 20). They violate their own rules of action; they do what they know to be wrong, their thoughts meanwhile accusing or else excusing one another. (See verse 15.) They practice those things that they condemn in others and thus pass sentence upon themselves (see verse 1), and for this they may be justly reprobated.

When People Are Rejected by God

When are men reprobated? In God's eyes, they are reprobated from eternity. But to men, they are reprobated when they become good for nothing. God knew from eternity how every event would be, how every sinner in the universe would behave himself. Because this was always present to His mind as much as it ever will be, His decision upon it all must have been from eternity. As far as making up His mind is concerned, He needs only to have all the evidence in the case, and this He has always had, as much as He ever will have. If, on the Day of Judgment, He will see cause to reprobate them and send them to hell, He has always seen this cause and has always been settled upon this subject. But as far as the reprobates themselves are concerned, they become reprobates when they stubbornly and finally refuse to accept eternal life on the terms of the Gospel.

In the mind of God, the doctrine of reprobation is just like the doctrine of election in this respect. Like all other purposes of the divine mind, it is eternal. God has no new thoughts, knowledge, purposes, or plans. In regard to us, reprobation is just like election because it is conditional. All other subjects in a man's life are fixed and already determined. God has set the bounds of man's habitation that he cannot pass, and all the circumstances of his life and death are settled. Even so, who does not know that the time of every man's death also depends on other factors, that his days may be lengthened or shortened by his own conduct, that years may be added to or subtracted from his life through his own doing?

The fact of a person's reprobation being settled in the mind of God does not alter the contingency with regard to us. It is to us just as much a matter of contingency as if neither God nor any being in the universe had any foreknowledge of the event. So, in regard to our salvation or damnation, although God is perfectly acquainted with what the result will be, still the event is just as dependent upon our own actions as if God knew nothing about it. The event alone develops to us what was before a certainty in the mind of God.

Why the Reprobate Were Created

Why did God create the reprobate? If God knew beforehand that such multitudes would sin and behave so wickedly that He would be obliged to cast them off forever, did He not create them on purpose to damn them? I answer no. He made them not to damn them, but for other, more important purposes. It is true that He knew they would be damned, and He created them in spite of this knowledge. He had other, weightier reasons for their creation. He created them for these beneficial reasons, not for the purpose of sending them to hell. So urgent were the reasons for their creation that He proceeded, despite the full knowledge of their frightful end.

There are many wise and benevolent purposes answered by the existence of reprobates, that we can discern. Undoubtedly, there are many other reasons with which we will be acquainted in the hereafter. In spite of the wicked intentions of reprobates, God makes use of them to do a great deal of good. The Devil himself has been an important agent in some of the most glorious transactions in the universe. But no thanks to him. When he put it into the heart of Judas to betray Christ, he obviously intended it for evil, but God meant it and overruled it for good. Neither the Devil nor Judas intended to glorify God or benefit mankind, but they actually were both concerned in slaying the very Cornerstone of man's salvation.

Wicked men are often in positions that are indispensable to the welfare of society. The existence of reprobates is indispensable to the existence of the elect, for they are often the parents of the elect; while they themselves are cast away in consequence of their rebellion, their children are often converted, sanctified, and saved. If the non-elect were never created, the elect could never live. In building up the kingdom of Christ, God often employs the hands of wicked men. To be sure, it is not their intention to build up the kingdom of God, but they put into motion such a train of events that, in the pursuit of their selfish ends, they are often instrumental in promoting His kingdom.

Suppose there is a wicked man who hates God and religion. He loves the world and gives his children a good education, desiring that they make a name for themselves, no matter how much injury they do to the cause of Christ. But God meets these children by His Spirit, converts and sanctifies them, and leads them to devote the hard earnings of their ungodly father to the building up and extension of His holy kingdom. This proves that *"the wealth of the sinner is stored up for the righteous"* (Proverbs 13:22).

Characteristics of Reprobation

Reprobation is just. Is it not just that God has allowed men to make their own choices, especially when the highest possible motivations are held out to them so that they will choose eternal life? Is it not just to reprobate men when they obstinately refuse salvation, when everything has been done that is consistent with infinite wisdom and benevolence to save them? Do not men choose to be either saved or lost? What will God do with you, sinner? You are unwilling to be saved. Why, then, should you object to being damned? If reprobation under these circumstances is not just, I challenge you, sinner, to tell me what is just.

Reprobation is the best thing that can be done for the universe, all things considered. Since the penalty of the law, although infinite, could not secure universal obedience under the wisest possible administration of moral government, and since multitudes of sinners will not be reclaimed and saved by the Gospel, one of three things must be done. Either moral government must be given up, the wicked must be annihilated, or they must be condemned and sent to hell.

Now, we will not even pretend that moral government should be given up. And annihilation would not be just, because it would not give sin what it justly deserves. But because sinners really deserve eternal death, and because their punishment may be of real value to the universe by creating respect for the authority of God and thus strengthening His government, it is plain that their condemnation and damnation is for the general good and makes the best use of the wicked that can be made.

Next, reprobation is impartial. It has always been found convenient, by those who oppose election and reprobation, to represent them as partial. If the word *partial* means that some are elected and others not, that some are reprobated and others not, then I have no objections to the term. But if *partial* means that any undue favor is directed toward one while it is removed from the other, if it means that God reprobated some rather than others on account of any prejudice or improper bias against them, then I utterly deny it and maintain that reprobation is entirely impartial. It is an impartial act that takes into account all the circumstances of the case and acts for the general good without any undue bias in favor of or against anyone. I have already shown that the reasons for reprobating sinners relate entirely to their own wickedness and the public interest—the public interest requiring their reprobation and damnation because they refuse to obey God.

Finally, reprobation is benevolent. It was benevolent of God to create men, though He foresaw that they would sin and become reprobates. If He foresaw that He could insure a certain amount of virtue and happiness that would counterbalance the sin and misery of those who would be lost, then certainly it was benevolent to create them. If the virtue and happiness that could be secured under a moral government would greatly surpass the incidental evils arising out of a defection of part of the subjects of this government, then a truly benevolent mind would choose to establish the government, despite the attendant evils.

Now, if those who are lost deserve their misery and bring it upon themselves by their own choice when they might have been saved, then certainly in their damnation there can be nothing inconsistent with justice or benevolence. God must have a moral government, or there can be no such thing as holiness in the created universe. For holiness in a creature is nothing less than a voluntary conformity to the government of God.

Undoubtedly, God views the loss of the soul as a great evil, and He always will look upon it as such and would gladly avoid the loss of every soul if it were consistent with the wisest administration of His government. How slanderous and offensive to God it must be, then, to say that He created sinners on purpose to damn them. He pours forth all the tender yearnings of a father over those whom He is obliged to destroy.

> *How can I give you up, Ephraim? How can I hand you over, Israel? How can I make you like Admah? How can I set you like Zeboiim? My heart churns within Me; My sympathy is stirred.* (Hosea 11:8)

And now, sinner, can you sit and find it in your heart to accuse the blessed God of a lack of benevolence? *"Serpents, brood of vipers! How can you escape the condemnation of hell?"* (Matthew 23:33).

Identifying the Reprobate

I will tell you how you may know who is reprobate. It may be difficult for us to ascertain with certainty in this world who is reprobate, but there are so many marks of condemnation given in the Bible that a sober and judicious investigation will give a rather correct opinion whether we or those around us are reprobates or not.

Prosperity in Sin

One evidence of reprobation is a long course of prosperity in sin. The psalmist put it this way in Psalm 92: *"When the wicked spring up like grass, and when all the workers of iniquity flourish, it is that they may be destroyed forever"* (verse 7). God often gives the wicked their portion in this world and lets them prosper and then lose everything at once. *"The wicked are reserved for the day of doom"* (Job 21:30). Therefore, where you see an individual prospering in his sins for a long time, there is reason to think that he is a reprobate.

Neglect of the Means of Grace

Habitual neglect of the means of grace is another mark of reprobation. If men are to be saved at all, it is through the sanctification of the Spirit and belief in the truth. Probably not one in ten thousand is saved of those who habitually absent themselves from places where God presents His claims. Sometimes a tract or the conversation or prayer of some friend will awaken an individual and lead him to the house of God. But, as a general fact, if a man stays away from the means of grace and neglects his Bible and the church, it is a fearful sign of reprobation and a sign that he will die in his sins. He is voluntary in it, and he does not neglect the means of grace because he is reprobate, but was reprobated because God foresaw that he would take this course.

Suppose a plague were in the land and was certain to prove fatal in every instance where the appropriate remedy was not applied. Now, if you wanted to know whose days were numbered and finished, and who among the sick were certain to die with the disease, would it not be those among them neglecting and despising the only appropriate remedy?

All this was known to God as certainly beforehand as afterwards. Now, if you wish to know who are reprobates in your city, or in any city, look at the multitude of Sabbath breakers, swearers, drunkards, and lechers. Look through the length and breadth of the land, and see the thousands of young men and women who are utterly neglecting and despising eternal salvation. Poor dying young people—not one in a thousand of them is likely to be saved!

Perhaps some of them came from a family of prayer, where they used to kneel morning and evening around the family altar. And now where are they, and where are they going? They are already within the sweep of the mighty whirlpool whose circling waters are drawing them nearer and nearer the roaring vortex. They engage in trifling activities. They do not heed the voice that cries from heaven, nor the wail that comes up from hell, but with accelerated motion, they circle round and round, until they are swallowed up and lost in the abyss of damnation.

Lack of the Spirit's Influence

You will see another sign of reprobation where people are entirely destitute of the strivings of the Spirit. I do not mean those who never heard the Gospel, but in gospel lands it is doubtful whether anyone lives without some of the strivings of the Holy Spirit, unless God has entirely abandoned him. Therefore, where the Spirit's strivings have entirely ceased with a soul, it is proof that this soul has been given up by God. God says, *"Yes, woe to them when I depart from them!"* (Hosea 9:12).

Repeated Resistance to Conversion

Where people have attended a revival and have not been converted, it is evidence that they are reprobates. This is not conclusive, but presumptive, evidence, and this presumption grows stronger and stronger every time an individual passes such a season without conversion. It is common for people, in seasons of revival, to have some conviction but to grieve away the Spirit. You may be one of these people, dreaming away one more offer of eternal salvation. If you have even once resisted the Spirit until He is quenched, I have little hope that anything I can write here will do any good. The great probability is that you will be lost.

Growing Old in Sin

Those who have grown old in sin are probably reprobates. It is a solemn and alarming fact that a vast majority of those who give evidence of piety are converted before they are twenty-five years old. Look at the history of revivals. Even in those that have had the greatest power, very few older people have been converted. Men who have made it their goal to attain worldly objects, who are determined to secure them before they will pay attention to religion and yield to the claims of the Maker, expecting afterwards to be converted, are almost always disappointed.

Such a cold calculation is odious in the sight of God. They take advantage of His leniency and say that, because He is merciful, they may continue in sin until they have secured their worldly objects and have worn themselves out in the service of the Devil. This disgusts their Maker, of course. You need not expect God to set His seal of approval upon such a calculation as this. He will not allow you to triumph, to say that you had served the Devil as long as you pleased and got to heaven at last.

As a man passes his twenty-fifth year, the probability of his conversion fearfully diminishes every year. Sinner, are you forty years old? Look over the list of people who have recently been converted in your community. How many among them are of your age? Perhaps some of you are fifty or sixty. You will seldom find one of your age converted. There is one here and there; they are few and far between, like beacons on distant mountaintops. Aged sinner, it is more than fifty chances to one that you are a reprobate.

Lack of Chastisements from God

Absence of chastisements is a sign of reprobation. God says in the epistle to the Hebrews,

> My son, do not despise the chastening of the LORD, nor be discouraged when you are rebuked by Him; for whom the LORD loves He chastens, and scourges every son whom He receives. If you endure chastening, God deals with you as with sons; for what son is there whom a father does not chasten? But if you are without chastening, of which all have become partakers, then you are illegitimate and not sons.   (Hebrews 12:5–8)

Lack of Reformation after Chastisement

When men are chastened and are not reformed by it, it is a mark of reprobation. A poet has said, "When pain cannot bless, heaven quits us in despair." God says of such, *"Why should you be stricken again? You will revolt more and more"* (Isaiah 1:5). When your afflictions are unsanctified, when you harden yourselves under His stripes, why should He not leave you to fill up the measure of your iniquity? (See Matthew 23:32.)

Embracing of Heresies

Embracing heresies is another mark of reprobation. Where individuals seem to be sold on believing a lie, there is solemn reason for fearing that they are among those upon whom God sends strong delusions. He allows them to believe a lie and be damned because they did not believe the truth but had pleasure in unrighteousness.

Where you see individuals giving themselves up to such delusions, the more honestly they believe them, the greater reason there is for believing that they are reprobates. The truth is so plain that, with the Bible in your hands, it is next to impossible to believe a fundamental heresy without being given up to the judicial curse of God. It is so hard to believe a lie with the truth of the Bible before you that the Devil cannot do it. Therefore, if you reject your Bible and embrace a fundamental falsehood, you are more stupid and overtaken by darkness than the Devil himself is. When a man professes to believe a lie, the only hope of his salvation that remains is that he does not sincerely believe it. Sinner, beware how you trifle with God's truth. How often have individuals begun to argue in favor of heresy, for the sake of argument and because they loved debate, until they have finally come to believe their own lies and are lost forever!

Remarks

1. *The salvation of reprobates is impossible only because they make it so, by their own wicked conduct.*

2. *God will turn the damnation of the reprobate to good account.* In establishing His government, He foresaw that great evils would occur, that multitudes would sin and persevere in rebellion until they were lost, despite all that could consistently be done to save them. God also foresaw that a vastly greater good would result from the virtue and happiness of holy beings, and that He could make good use even of the punishment of the wicked.

I do not mean that the damnation of the wicked results in greater good than their salvation would if they would repent. If their salvation could be secured by any means that would agree with the highest good of the universe, it would be greatly preferred. But, as this cannot be, God will do the best that can be done in this case. When He cannot save them, He will, by their punishment, erect a monument to His justice, lay its foundation deep in hell, and build it up to heaven, so that the smoke of their torment may forever stand as a memento of the hatefulness and punishment of sin.

3. *It is very wicked and blasphemous to complain about God when He has done the best that infinite wisdom, benevolence, and power could do.* Who will complain? Surely not the elect; they have no reason to complain. Will the reprobate complain, when he has actually forced God either to give up His government or to send him to hell?

4. *Reprobates are bound to praise God.* Sinners, God has created you and given you many blessings; He offers you eternal life. Will you refuse to praise Him?

5. *God has every reason to complain about you, sinner.* How much good you might do! See how much good individuals have often done! Now, you rob God of all the good you might do. While eternity rolls, on how many errands of love might you go, diffusing happiness to the utmost bounds of Jehovah's empire? But you refuse to obey Him; you are in league with hell and prefer to

scatter *"firebrands, arrows, and death"* (Proverbs 26:18), to destroy your own soul, and to lead others to perdition with you. You drive on and help to set in motion all the elements of rebellion in earth and hell. Will you complain about God? He has reason to complain about you. He is the injured party. He has created you, has held you in His hand, and has given you breath. In return, you have breathed out rebellion, blasphemy, and contempt of God. You have compelled Him to pronounce you reprobate.

6. *There is reason to believe that there are many reprobates in the church.* This is the probable history of many who claim to be religious: they had convictions of sin, and after a while their distress, more or less, suddenly abated. When their convictions left them, they thought that perhaps this was conversion; this very "perhaps" created a sensation of pleasure, and they became confident that this pleasure was evidence that they were converted. As their confidence increased, their joy at the thought of being saved also increased. This selfish joy has been the foundation upon which they have built their hopes for eternity. Now you see them in the church, transacting business upon worldly principles, making excuses for sin, and finding a thousand justifications for conformity to the world. They live on in sin, perhaps not openly wicked, but negligent of duty, and go down to hell from within the church.

7. *Reprobates live to fill up the measure of their iniquity.* The Amorites were spared, not because there was any hope of their reformation but because their cup of iniquity was *"not yet complete"* (Genesis 15:16). Christ said to the Jews, *"Fill up, then, the measure of your fathers' guilt"* (Matthew 23:32), and God said to Pharaoh, *"For this purpose I have raised you up, that I may show My power in you"* (Exodus 9:16). Oh, dreadful thought—to live to fill up the measure of your sins! The *"cup of trembling"* (Isaiah 51:17) and of *"indignation"* (Revelation 14:10) is also filling up with *"the wine of the wrath of God"* (verse 10), which will be *"poured out* [to

you] *full strength*" (Revelation 14:10), when there will be no one to deliver you. Remember, your "*judgment has not been idle, and [your] destruction does not slumber*" (2 Peter 2:3).

8. *Saints should not envy sinners.* The psalmist once had this trial. He said,

> *Truly God is good to Israel, to such as are pure in heart. But as for me, my feet had almost stumbled; my steps had nearly slipped. For I was envious of the boastful, when I saw the prosperity of the wicked. For there are no pangs in their death, but their strength is firm. They are not in trouble as other men, nor are they plagued like other men....When I thought how to understand this, it was too painful for me; until I went into the sanctuary of God; then I understood their end. Surely You set them in slippery places; You cast them down to destruction. Oh, how they are brought to desolation, as in a moment! They are utterly consumed with terrors.*   (Psalm 73:1–5, 16–19)

How can a Christian envy them, standing upon a slippery slope, with fiery billows rolling beneath them? "*Their foot shall slip in due time*" (Deuteronomy 32:35). Christians, don't envy the wicked, though they enjoy the wealth of the world. Do not envy them; they are poor creatures! Their time is short; they have almost had all their good things.

Some of you, my readers, have not in the least benefited from anything I have said or could say. You have set yourselves in opposition to God and have taken such an attitude that truth never reaches you to do you good. Now, sinner, if you do this and continue in this state of mind, later on you will have additional evidence that God has given you up and that you are a reprobate. Will you continue in your sins under these circumstances? Don't talk of the doctrine of election or reprobation as being in your way. No man is ever reprobated for any other reason than that he is an obstinate sinner.

Have you been reading this to find something that you can stumble over? Take care; if you wish to raise objections, you can always find enough opportunities for that. Sinners have stumbled into hell over every other doctrine of the Bible, and you may stumble over this.

What would you think of a man who read this book and then hung himself, saying that he did it because God foreknew that he would do it and that God, by creating him with this foreknowledge, intended for him to do it? Would saying that excuse him? No.

Sinner, you only show that you are determined to harden your heart, resist God, and thus compel the holy Lord God to reject you. There is no doctrine of the Bible that can save you if you persevere in sin, and none that can damn you if you repent and embrace the Gospel. The blood of Christ flows freely. The fountain is open. Sinner, will you have eternal life? Will you have it now, or will you reject it? Will you trample the law underfoot (see Hebrews 10:29) and stumble over the Gospel to the depths of hell?

Twelve

The Love of the World

*Do not love the world or the things in the world. If anyone
loves the world, the love of the Father is not in him.*
—1 John 2:15

What is meant by "the love of the world"? The love of the
world that is spoken of in the above verse is not every kind or
degree of desire for worldly objects. Human nature is such that
a certain amount, and certain kinds, of worldly objects are indispensable to our existence. We need food and clothing, means of
making a living, as well as various worldly things. The proper
desire of these things is not sinful or inconsistent with the love
of God.

But to love the world is to make worldly things the principal objects of desire and pursuit. To love them and desire them
more than to love God and man, to be more anxious to obtain
them, to spend more time in their acquisition than in efforts
to glorify God and save the souls of men, is to love the world
in the sense of the text verse. Where the love of God and of
men is supreme in the heart, there may be a proper desire for
worldly objects; but where an individual prefers the acquisition of wealth or of worldly objects above glorifying God and
doing good to men, it is certain that the love of the world is
supreme in his heart.

Those Who Love the World Supremely

Those Who Cheat and Defraud Others

What sort of person loves the world in this manner? First, all who cheat and defraud to obtain the things of the world. I do not need any evidence to prove that a man who will cheat and defraud his neighbor does not love him as he does himself. It is self-evident that a man who will disobey God for the purpose of obtaining worldly goods does not love God supremely. Indeed, that he loves the things of the world supremely is a simple matter of fact.

Those with Mostly Worldly Cares

Second, all those whose anxieties and cares are mostly about worldly things have the love of the world in them. If they are more concerned for the things of the world, more anxious and earnest in the pursuit of them than in glorifying God and in doing good to men, they love the world supremely.

But you may object and say, "May a man not be anxious to obtain worldly things so that he may do good with his money?" I answer that it is absurd to suppose that a man whose supreme goal is to glorify God and do good to man would concern himself principally with worldly things. It is the end that gives value to the means. It is the end that is the main object of thought and of desire; and to suppose that a man's anxieties and cares would focus on the means of bringing about the end, rather than on the end itself, is absurd and impossible.

Suppose a gentleman is engaged to be married and has commenced a journey for that purpose. His heart is greatly set upon the end he has in view. Is it likely that either the delights or cares of his journey will occupy more of his thoughts and absorb more of his emotions than the purpose for which he has undertaken the journey? I think it would be obvious to most people that, in such a case, this man would pass from stage to stage of his journey hardly conscious of the incidents that occurred along the way. His bride and his marriage would fill up his thoughts by day and be the subject of his dreams by night. He would desire to complete his journey more rapidly only to more speedily accomplish his heart's desire.

And now, what about a man who loves God supremely and whose desire for money and for worldly goods is that he may glorify God and benefit mankind? Can he be so anxious and so busy about the means as to lose sight of the end? Will his interest in the end be swallowed up in efforts to obtain the means? This cannot be.

And now, you who practice fraud and take advantage of the ignorance of men, you who cheat them in little or great things, do you pretend to love God? If so, you are extreme hypocrites. And you who are filled with cares about worldly things, whose time, thoughts, and emotions are swallowed up in efforts to obtain them, you may be assured that you love the world and that the love of God is not in you.

Those Who Care Only for Themselves

Third, the love of the world is in all those who consult only their own interests in the transaction of business. God requires you to *"love your neighbor as yourself"* (Leviticus 19:18). He also says, *"Let each of you look out not only for his own interests, but also for the interests of others"* (Philippians 2:4), and *"Let no man seek his own, but every man another's wealth"* (1 Corinthians 10:24 KJV). These are requirements of God; they are the very spirit and substance of the Gospel. Benevolence is a desire to do good to others. A willingness to deny self, for the purpose of promoting the interests of your neighbor, is the very Spirit of Christ; it is the heart and soul of His Gospel.

Suppose a man, in his transactions with others, aims only at promoting his own interests. He seeks his own wealth, and he does not consider the welfare of others. He does not aim at benefiting the individual with whom he transacts business; his only objective is to take care of himself. This is the very opposite of the spirit of the Gospel. Does this man love his neighbor as himself? Does he supremely love the God who has prohibited all selfishness, on pain of eternal death? No! If he loved God, he would not disobey Him for the sake of making money.

If he loved his neighbor as himself, if he felt that it was more blessed to give than to receive (Acts 20:35), if he had the spirit of the Gospel, he would of course feel as great a desire for the interests of those with whom he deals as he does for himself. He would be as anxious to give as to get a good bargain, if not more so. Self-denial, in order to promote the happiness and the interests of others, would be his joy, would constitute his happiness, would be that to which he would be inclined.

Can you, my readers, deny this principle? What is your spiritual state? Do you have the love of God in you? How do you transact business? Do you consult the interests of those with whom you deal as much as you do your own? Or in all your transactions, do you aim simply at securing a profit for yourself? If you do the latter, the love of God is not in you. You do not have any piety in your heart.

Those Who Are Upset When Others Prosper

Fourth, the love of the world is in all those who feel chagrined and grieved when they find that the person with whom they have dealt has the best of the bargain and has made a greater profit than themselves. Now, if a man had the Spirit of Christ, he would rejoice in this. It would be the thing at which he would aim: to benefit the individual with whom he deals as much as possible. If he afterward learned that the other party greatly benefited by the bargain, it would gratify him all the more.

Now, how is it with you, my readers? Do you find yourselves gratified and delighted when you find that you have greatly contributed to the interests of those with whom you deal, in having given them the best side of the bargain? Be honest; see whether you love your neighbor as yourself; see whether you love God supremely. He requires you to seek your neighbor's wealth instead of your own, to look out for the interests of others as well as your own. Do you have the Spirit of the God who lays down this rule of action? If not, you do not have the love of God in you.

Those Who Do Business Only for Profit

Fifth, the love of the world is in all those who will make deals only when they can make a profit. There are many who will deal only when they can promote their own interests, no matter how much it might benefit anybody else. The interests of the individual who desires to make the bargain with them are not taken into account at all. They do not think of making a bargain to benefit others, and they will turn away from the proposal instantly if they cannot promote their own selfish ends. They will be very accommodating, kind, and attentive while there is any prospect of making a good profit, but the negotiation is broken off instantly, without courtesy or good manners, whenever they can make nothing by the bargain. This shows that they do not consider the interests of those with whom they deal, and that the world is their god.

Those Who Take Advantage of Others' Ignorance

Sixth, all those who will take advantage of the ignorance of those with whom they deal, to get a good bargain out of them, love the world supremely. Cases of this kind occur quite often. A customer comes in. He is instantly looked over from head to toe by every eye, to see whether he understands the value of the articles he wishes to purchase. He is surveyed to see whether it will be difficult or easy to get a good bargain out of him, whether it will do to set the price of goods high—and how high—and whether it is likely that he will buy much or little. And if he wishes to spend a lot of money, the first things that he asks about are priced low, so that he will be led to buy even more by thinking that all the articles are priced low. This is supreme selfishness, fraud, and the very opposite of the Spirit of Christ. For such a man to profess the love of God is obvious hypocrisy.

Those Who Knowingly Sell Useless and Harmful Items

Seventh, those who will sell useless articles to men for the sake of profit do not have the love of God in them. A man who does this cannot be considering the interest of his neighbor at all. He must be acting on principles of pure selfishness. He takes the money and agrees that it should be spent *"for what is not bread, and...for what does not satisfy"* (Isaiah 55:2). This is the direct opposite of the Spirit of Christ.

Some people will sell items that are not only useless, but also harmful, because they are designed to promote the pride and vanity of men, to take their hearts from God, and to fasten them upon the trifles of this vain world. These people tempt the deceitful hearts of men and enlist them in the chase of fashion, gaiety, and worldliness. Now, instead of being pious, they who do this take the Devil's place and tempt mankind to sin.

All who sell harmful items for the sake of profit do not have the love of God in them. The man who will sell articles that he knows will cause harm to his fellowmen, for the sake of gain, has the very spirit of hell. How can a man pretend to love God when he will deal out death and damnation to men and make them pay for it, thereby not only poisoning them to death, but also robbing them of their money? It is shameful. You hypocrite! You wretch! You are an enemy of God and man, a wolf in sheep's clothing. (See Matthew 7:15.) Lay aside your mask, and write the name "Satan" on your door.

Those Who Do Business Selfishly

Eighth, all those who transact business upon principles of supreme selfishness, rather than on principles of benevolence, love the world supremely. The principles of supreme selfishness have been established by selfish men for selfish purposes, without even the pretense of conformity to the law of love. Upon these principles it is neither demanded nor expected that anyone should seek another's wealth, but that everyone should take care of himself, should purchase as low and sell as high as he can, and should do all he can to promote his own interests. Can a man love God supremely, and his neighbor as himself, when he daily and habitually transacts business upon the principles of selfishness, which are founded in the direct opposite of the requirement of God? In such business transactions, self is the beginning, the middle, and the end of the whole matter.

Those Who Use All Their Money for Worldly Causes

Ninth, all those who engage in business, to the neglect of spiritual exercises, love the world supremely. Many who profess to be religious seem just about as much determined to do good with their money as impenitent sinners are to repent. They claim to engage in business for the glory of God, but instead of using their money for this purpose, they enlarge their capital and their business, and transact business upon the principles of worldly men. Thus they are constantly deluded. Instead of contributing their money as they go along toward the building up of the kingdom of Jesus Christ, they add their yearly profits to their capital, until nearly all their time, thoughts, and emotions are engrossed with moneymaking. Now, you who practice this, why do you not see that you are deceiving yourselves?

The only way in which money can be used for the glory of God and the good of men, is to promote the spirituality and holiness of men. If you pursue business in a way that is inconsistent with your own spirituality, you might as well talk of getting drunk or swearing for the glory of God. For you to neglect communion with God under the pretense of making money for Him is sheer hypocrisy. If you prefer business above prayer, if you busy yourselves in your offices, shops, and businesses and neglect your prayer closets, the love of God is not in you. To pretend that you love God is just as absurd as to suppose that your eagerness to make money for the glory of God leads you to neglect communion with Him, or that your great zeal to serve Him and great love for Him leads you to neglect communion with Him.

Those Who Neglect Church in order to Make Money

Tenth, those who make their business an excuse for not attending church and using other means for the conversion of sinners, have the love of the world in them. It is obvious that such individuals are not transacting business for God. The only possible use of making money for the glory of God is to use it for the conversion and sanctification of sinners. This is the great purpose of doing business for God. But to be so busy in making money that you neglect to make direct and personal efforts for the conversion of sinners is absurd. It proves that the purpose of making money is not to convert, sanctify, and save sinners; in such cases, it is clear that money is sought for the love of it, not for the purpose of building up the kingdom of Jesus Christ.

Those Whose Business Distracts Them from God

Eleventh, all those whose business diverts their thoughts and emotions from God have the love of the world in them. If they were transacting business for God, the busier and more engaged they were in His service, in doing His will, and in making money for Him, the more He would be present in all their thoughts, and the deeper their piety would be.

Those Who Are Rich

Twelfth, all rich men love the world supremely. Jesus Christ said, *"It is easier for a camel to go through the eye of a needle than for a rich man to enter the kingdom of God"* (Matthew 19:24). You say, "Yes, this is true, if he sets his heart upon his riches." But what I affirm is that every rich man does set his heart upon his riches. If he did not, he would not be rich. If he loved the kingdom of God supremely, he would give his riches to promote that kingdom. We always do what we choose to do. If you have money and you see furniture or a dress or anything else that you would like to have, you are certain to make the exchange of your money for it, if it is in your power.

Therefore, when a rich man's money can be but is not used under the Gospel for the glory of God and the conversion of souls, it is absolute proof that he loves the world supremely. To say that he is rich but does not set his heart upon riches, that he continues to retain his wealth and yet does not set his heart upon it, is absurd and false. For certainly, nothing but a supreme attachment to it could cause him to hold on to it, when every wind is loaded down with cries to send the Bread of Life to those who are ready to perish.

But perhaps some will say that much depends upon the instruction that rich people have received, that they believe that they may lawfully retain and enjoy their wealth. This does not relieve the difficulty, however, for the question is not what they may lawfully do, but what they are inclined to do. Suppose an affectionate wife has a husband in captivity whom she tenderly loves. The price of his ransom is fixed, and she, with her earnings and savings, is determined to pay the price. Of what use is it to tell her that she may lawfully purchase clothing and items of convenience, and that it is lawful for her to have the comforts of life? Will she lay out her money for these things? No, she will scarcely allow herself a pair of shoes. She will practice the most rigid economy and will take a satisfaction in denying herself everything but the absolutely necessities of life, until she has saved the sum demanded for her husband's ransom.

It is of no use to preach to this woman about the lawfulness of using her money for other purposes. She has one all-absorbing purpose in mind. She values money only as it will contribute to the promotion of this objective. Any instruction concerning the lawfulness of using her money for other purposes will have no effect on her practice. Every penny that she can spare is laid out for the promotion of this object of her heart's desire. Likewise, if a man loves God supremely, if he longs for the coming and prosperity of God's kingdom more than for anything else, the question with him will not be whether he may lawfully enjoy riches. The truth is, even if he could enjoy them lawfully, it is not his choice to do it. He prefers to build up the kingdom of Christ with his money, and he considers his money valueless unless it can contribute to this purpose.

Therefore, I consider it to be a certain truth that if a man is rich and continues to be rich under the Gospel, he must prefer wealth above the promotion of the kingdom of Jesus Christ. You may object and say that Abraham, Job, David, and Solomon were rich. But the command had never been given in their day to *"preach the gospel to every creature"* (Mark 16:15), and there is no reason for believing that they so much as dreamed that the world could be converted in the way in which we now know that it can and must be converted. They could not, therefore, have had the same motives for using their wealth for the conversion of the world that we have. Therefore, if they kept their wealth, it was no certain sign that they preferred it before the kingdom and glory of God.

Those Who Give God the Leftovers

Thirteenth, a man who gives God his surplus income, yet practices no self-denial, gives what costs him nothing and provides no substantial evidence that he loves God. If he gratifies all his desires and the desires of his family, if he provides for them all the comforts and conveniences of life, and gives to God only what remains of his income over and above his expenditures, he really practices no self-denial. He enjoys all that can be enjoyed of wealth, and is really ridding himself of the trouble of taking care of it by giving the balance of his yearly income to the cause of Christ. This is much like a safety valve to let off the surplus steam that would otherwise burst the boiler.

Some of you may object and ask, "Should every man give up all his capital and means at once for promoting the cause of Christ?" This might not be Christian economy. A man's capital, if it is not larger than is necessary for the wisest transaction of business, is to be considered in light of tools with which he serves God and his generation. In such cases, if he gives from his income after deducting the necessary expenses of his family, I cannot see that such a use of it is inconsistent with the love of God. But for a man to live and die rich, to hoard up his income and enjoy his wealth, is the psalmist's definition of a wicked man who has his *"portion in this life"* (Psalm 17:14).

Those Who Are Most Interested in Money

Fourteenth, all those who are more interested in secular news that relates to money transactions, than in the accounts of revivals of religion and in those things that pertain more particularly to the kingdom of Christ, love the world supremely. Show me a man who is looking over the secular news, noting the price of stocks and concentrating on questions of money speculations, but who does not read or take an interest in reports of revivals and the onward movements of the church. If he claims to love God, his claim is utter hypocrisy.

Some who profess to be religious get all excited when great money speculations are to be made. When stocks are high or when real estate is on the rise, they get excited about any opportunity to make money. But if an effort is made to promote a revival of religion, they are too busy in their speculations to give their time and hearts to it. They may pretend that they are making money for God, but they have no heart to engage in directly promoting the end at which they aim. The plain truth is that, if they prefer opportunities to make money over revivals of religion, they love money and love the world supremely.

Those Who Are Most Affected by a Loss of Money

Fifteenth, all those who are more affected by a loss of money than they are by the low state of religion and the state of dying sinners, love the world supremely. This needs neither proof nor illustration.

Those Who Break God's Law for the Sake of Money

Sixteenth, all those who disobey the commandments of God for the purpose of making or saving money, love the world supremely. Those who would seek to acquire or hold on to money rather than obey God's laws certainly love money supremely. Should we not realize that any property in our possession belongs to God? How could we consider violating the Sabbath in an effort to gain a few dollars?

Those Who Are Not Most Gratified by Giving Money to God

Seventeenth, all those who do not feel more gratified by using money for the cause of Christ than any other use of it, love the world supremely. Take again the case of the woman who is earning money to relieve her husband from bondage. What other use can she make of money that would so much gratify her heart? In her estimation, it is this purpose that gives value to money. If someone were to give her a purse full of gold, would she say, "Now I can buy myself a nice dress" or "Now I can furnish my house and live fashionably"? No, but bursting into tears of joy and gratitude, she would exclaim, "Now I can redeem my husband!"

It is the same with a man who loves God and longs for the coming of His kingdom. He will feel most gratified when using money for the promotion of this purpose. Jesus Christ has said, *"It is more blessed to give than to receive"* (Acts 20:35). The truly benevolent man has the highest and holiest pleasure in disposing of his possessions to promote the glory of God and the good of his fellowmen. Instead of giving to those purposes grudgingly, he will unsparingly pour out of his treasures with the fullest, readiest heart. His heart longs for this. He therefore considers nothing a sacrifice that is used for promoting Christ's kingdom.

Those Who Prefer Moneymaking above Giving to God

Eighteenth, all those who prefer opportunities to make money above a contribution for the promotion of the interests of Christ's kingdom, love the world supremely. If they loved God supremely, they would desire to take advantage of the moneymaking opportunity only for the purpose of enabling them to make the contribution. If they made a hundred or a thousand dollars, they would say, "Now I wish I had an opportunity to use this money toward the

The Love of the World 239

cause of Christ." But if they love the moneymaking itself and are not ready and joyful in the contribution, then they love the world and do not have the love of God in them.

Those Who Prefer Receiving above Giving

Nineteenth, all those who do not really enjoy giving more than receiving love the world supremely. If they loved God supremely, their supreme joy in receiving would be that they might immediately turn around and give to the cause of Christ. But if they wish always to receive and do not enjoy the giving of money as they do the receiving of it, it must be because they love the world.

Those Who Are Most Frugal Regarding the Church

Lastly, all those who are more frugal in their expenditures for the kingdom of Christ than in their expenditures upon themselves and their families, love the world supremely. There are multitudes of professedly pious people who seem to think it a Christian duty to buy only the cheapest things for the worship and service of God, while in their own homes and for themselves and their families they practice a very different principle. If a church is to be decorated, these people insist that everything must be done with as little expense as possible. If there are carpets, they must be of the cheapest kind. If there are cushions, lights, or other conveniences, almost anything will do, provided it is cheap. Things are allowed to be out of order; dust is allowed to accumulate, and the house of God is permitted to waste away. And all this is done under the pious pretense of Christian economy.

Many churches have no lights, many have no furnaces, and others have broken windows and doors that are so dilapidated that they will scarcely shut. Others have rotting staircases, and the church is either not painted at all or is so faded that you would suppose it the abode of the drunkard if it were a residential home. Many churches have no carpets, while carpets are more needed in churches than in any other building in order to prevent the disturbance that always occurs when people are going and coming on an uncarpeted floor. There are many people who are entirely unwilling to pay the expense of furnishing a house of worship as they furnish their own dwellings.

Now, whatever the pretense may be and however such things may be baptized by the name of Christian economy, all such conduct has its foundation in the love of the world and in supreme selfishness. People are always free in using their money to promote the causes dearest to their hearts. Therefore, if our hearts are set supremely upon honoring God with our substance, it is certain that if in anything we are bountiful and liberal in our expenditures, it will be in furnishing places for His worship and for all that is essential to decency, comfort, and enjoyment in His service.

Why Such People Cannot Love God

Having noticed some of the principal evidences of supreme attachment to the world, I now proceed to suggest several reasons why such individuals cannot love God. The text verse expresses a very strong negative: *"If anyone loves the world,"* said the apostle, *"the love of the Father is not in him."* This is the language and the doctrine of the whole Bible. As far as Scripture testimony goes, the proof is conclusive. But let me mention several considerations that will prove beyond all doubt that individuals upon whom these marks of worldliness are found do not have the love of God in them.

First, it is impossible for a man to have two supreme objects of affection. Christ said, *"No one can serve two masters; for either he will hate the one and love the other, or else he will be loyal to the one and despise the other"* (Matthew 6:24). If he has any acceptable love for God, it must be supreme. To say that a man loves the world in the sense of the text verse, and that he loves God with any acceptable love, is a contradiction. It is the same as saying that he loves both God and the world supremely.

Second, a man cannot love two objects at the same time that are entirely opposed to each other. The apostle John immediately added to the text verse, *"For all that is in the world; the lust of the flesh, the lust of the eyes, and the pride of life; is not of the Father but is of the world"* (1 John 2:16). The love of the world and the love of God are entirely opposite states of mind, so that to exercise them both at the same time is impossible.

Third, the apostle Paul declared that minding the flesh is enmity against God. (See Romans 8:5–7.)

Lastly, it is supreme selfishness, which is the direct opposite of the love of God and man. Simply naming these considerations is proof enough that *"if anyone loves the world, the love of the Father is not in him."*

Remarks

1. *You can see from this subject that if men would transact worldly business according to the principles of the Gospel, it would be infinitely better for the world in every respect.* If everyone sought to promote the happiness and interests of others, the amount of property, and of every other item, would be greatly increased. Some people seem to think that unless they think only of their own interests, it is impossible for society to exist. "What!" they say. "Would you have us all seek not our own interests, but the interests of others? What, then, would become of our own interests?" I answer that your interests would be secured if, while you were careful to benefit others, they were just as careful to benefit you. In this way, the

spirit that would be cherished and cultivated by this course of conduct would shed a sweet, healing, and refreshing influence over all the discord and disquietude of selfishness. Peace, love, and heaven would reign in the hearts of men.

But you may object and say that worldly men will not practice these principles, so it is impossible that Christians should practice them without giving up all the business of the world into their hands. This is a radical and ruinous mistake. Suppose it were known that Christians universally discarded all selfishness in their business and acted upon principles of entire benevolence, that in all their dealings they sought the interests of those with whom they deal. Worldly men would immediately be forced to transact business upon these principles or give up all the business of the world into the hands of Christians. For who would deal with men who acted upon principles of supreme selfishness, when he might just as well transact business with those who would treat him not only with equity, but also with entire benevolence?

Thus, it is perfectly within the power of the church to compel worldly men to transact business according to Gospel principles, or not transact it at all. And woe to the church if she does not reverse and annihilate the whole system of doing business according to principles of selfishness!

Perhaps some of you will say, "If this doctrine is true, then who can be saved?" Certainly not those who manage their affairs according to principles that are in direct opposition to the benevolence of the Gospel. Nor can they be saved who make selfishness the rule of their lives and satisfy themselves with being honest in this sense of honesty, instead of being governed by the law of love. Those who seek their own, and not their neighbor's wealth, who mind earthly things and consider it more blessed to receive than to give, have the love of the world in them. If there is any truth in the Word of God, all such men are on the way to hell.

Others may object and say, "This is very uncharitable. If this is true, nearly everyone in the church is a hypocrite." My answer to this is that the doctrine is true, whatever your interpretation may be. I do not pretend to be more charitable than God is, nor do I expect that there is any piety in those of whom God has said that His love is not in them. I will not be charitable enough to throw away my Bible, or to suppose that the lovers of the world are the friends of God. Multitudes of so-called Christians are deceived; they love the world supremely. And because the great mass of professing Christians are of this state of mind, we are not to dispute our Bibles and charitably hope that such people may be saved.

2. *You see from this subject why so few who claim to be religious have a spirit of prayer.* The truth is, the love of God is not in them. Look around you. Nearly everyone is in pursuit of worldly gain. The principles upon which almost all business is transacted are those of supreme selfishness. How, then, can a spirit of prayer prevail among these people? These same principles prevail almost universally through the country. Men and women of every occupation, without hesitation, transact their business according to selfish principles and seek their own and not their neighbor's wealth. It is impossible for the love of God to prevail in the church, or in any heart, while people are motivated by such principles.

3. *You see from this subject why young converts so uniformly grow cold in religion.* An individual who passes through one business season, acting according to worldly business principles, will find that the love of God cannot possibly be alive in his heart. He assiduously cultivates and cherishes a spirit of selfishness, and in all his work he does not so much as intend to seek the good of others, but he seeks only his own good. Therefore, the reasons for such universal backsliding are quite obvious.

4. *From this subject, you can see that the religion of most people in the church is not the religion of love but of fear.* They fear the Lord

but serve their own gods. Their consciences drag them along in the dry performance of what they call duty. They have a dry, legal, earthly spirit, and their pretended service is hypocrisy and utter wickedness.

5. *You can see from this subject why so little is actually accomplished by all the means that are used for the building up of the kingdom of Jesus Christ.* Men would much rather give their money than live holy lives and walk with God. There seems to be an effort now to convert the world with money. Professedly pious men enter into moneymaking opportunities; and while their hearts, souls, and lives are absorbed in the spirit of this world, they are trying to persuade themselves that their money will be a substitute for a holy life and will compensate for the neglect of personal exertions to save the souls of men. But you may be sure that God will teach them their mistake.

The spontaneous conduct of the early church showed what true piety will do in leading men to renounce the world. While the love of God pervaded the church, men were moved by principles different from those of commercial justice. They sought not their own, but the things of Jesus Christ.

But you may ask, "Is nearly everyone in the church wrong, then?" On this subject they are wrong. In most things, the church of the present day is orthodox in theory but vastly heretical in practice. It is nothing new for the church to be nearly all wrong. More than once or twice nearly the entire church has departed from God and satisfied herself with the religion of selfishness.

You who are convicted of worldliness, I beg you not to finish this book and say that you hope that you love God, despite the fact that some or nearly all of these evidences are against you. I declare to you, before God and the Lord Jesus Christ, that if these marks of worldliness are upon you, the love of God is not in you.

Do not be deceived, God is not mocked; for whatever a man sows, that he will also reap. For he who sows to his flesh will of the flesh reap corruption, but he who sows to the Spirit will of the Spirit reap everlasting life. (Galatians 6:7–8)

About the Author

Charles G. Finney (1792–1875) was a man with a message that burned through the religious deadwood and secular darkness of his time. He had the ability to shock both saint and sinner alike. Because he was radical in both his methods and his message, Finney was criticized for almost everything except being boring.

Born in Connecticut in 1792, Finney was nearly thirty years of age when he turned from his skepticism regarding Christianity and wholeheartedly embraced the Bible as the true Word of God. He gave up his law profession in order to spread the gospel, and he soon became the most noteworthy revivalist of the nineteenth century, one of the leaders of the Second Great Awakening. It is estimated that over 250,000 souls were converted as a result of his preaching. While Finney carried his revivals to several middle and eastern states, the bulk of his meetings were in New York towns, especially Rome, Rochester, Utica, Clinton, Antwerp, Evans' Mills, Western, and Gouverneur.

In 1832, Finney began pastoring Second Free Presbyterian Church in New York City. In 1835, upon the request of Arthur Tappan, Finney established the theology department at Oberlin Collegiate Institute (today known as Oberlin College). He served there as a professor of theology, as well as pastor of Oberlin's First Congregational Church, until a few years before his death. He was also a member of the Oberlin College Board of Trustees from 1846 until he was elected president in 1851. During these years, he continued to carry on his evangelism, even visiting Great Britain twice in 1849–50 and 1859–60.

Finney was married three times in his life, first to Lydia Root Andrews (m. 1824), then to Elizabeth Ford Atkinson (m. 1848), and then to Rebecca Allen Rayl (m. 1865). All three of these women assisted Finney in his evangelistic efforts, accompanying him on his revival tours during their lives. In August 1875, Finney died in Oberlin due to a heart ailment.

www.ingramcontent.com/pod-product-compliance
Lightning Source LLC
Chambersburg PA
CBHW071417090426
42737CB00011B/1497